SQA

Official

SQA

Past Papers

WITH ANSWERS

Higher
Mathematics

2010–2014

HODDER
GIBSON
AN HACHETTE UK COMPANY

Hodder Gibson is grateful to the copyright holders, as credited on the final page of the Question Section, for permission to use their material. Every effort has been made to trace the copyright holders and to obtain their permission for the use of copyright material. Hodder Gibson will be happy to receive information allowing us to rectify any error or omission in future editions.

Hachette UK's policy is to use papers that are natural, renewable and recyclable products and made from wood grown in sustainable forests. The logging and manufacturing processes are expected to conform to the environmental regulations of the country of origin.

Orders: please contact Bookpoint Ltd, 130 Park Drive, Abingdon, Oxon OX14 4SE. Telephone: (44) 01235 827720. Fax: (44) 01235 400454.

Lines are open 9.00–5.00, Monday to Saturday, with a 24-hour message answering service. Visit our website at www.hoddereducation.co.uk. Hodder Gibson can be contacted direct on: Tel: 0141 848 1609; Fax: 0141 889 6315; email: hoddergibson@hodder.co.uk

This collection first published in 2014 by

Hodder Gibson, an imprint of Hodder Education,

An Hachette UK Company

2a Christie Street

Paisley PA1 1NB

BrightRED   Hodder Gibson is grateful to Bright Red Publishing Ltd for collaborative work in preparation of this book and all
PUBLISHING   SQA Past Paper, National 5 and Higher for CfE Model Paper titles 2014.

Typeset by PDQ Digital Media Solutions Ltd, Bungay, Suffolk NR35 1BY

Printed in the UK

A catalogue record for this title is available from the British Library

ISBN 978-1-4718-3685-5

3 2 1

2015 2014

Introduction

Study Skills – what you need to know to pass exams!

Pause for thought

Many students might skip quickly through a page like this. After all, we all know how to revise. Do you really though?

Think about this:

"IF YOU ALWAYS DO WHAT YOU ALWAYS DO, YOU WILL ALWAYS GET WHAT YOU HAVE ALWAYS GOT."

Do you like the grades you get? Do you want to do better? If you get full marks in your assessment, then that's great! Change nothing! This section is just to help you get that little bit better than you already are.

There are two main parts to the advice on offer here. The first part highlights fairly obvious things but which are also very important. The second part makes suggestions about revision that you might not have thought about but which WILL help you.

Part 1

DOH! It's so obvious but …

Start revising in good time

Don't leave it until the last minute – this will make you panic.

Make a revision timetable that sets out work time AND play time.

Sleep and eat!

Obvious really, and very helpful. Avoid arguments or stressful things too – even games that wind you up. You need to be fit, awake and focused!

Know your place!

Make sure you know exactly **WHEN and WHERE** your exams are.

Know your enemy!

Make sure you know what to expect in the exam.

How is the paper structured?

How much time is there for each question?

What types of question are involved?

Which topics seem to come up time and time again?

Which topics are your strongest and which are your weakest?

Are all topics compulsory or are there choices?

Learn by DOING!

There is no substitute for past papers and practice papers – they are simply essential! Tackling this collection of papers and answers is exactly the right thing to be doing as your exams approach.

Part 2

People learn in different ways. Some like low light, some bright. Some like early morning, some like evening / night. Some prefer warm, some prefer cold. But everyone uses their BRAIN and the brain works when it is active. Passive learning – sitting gazing at notes – is the most INEFFICIENT way to learn anything. Below you will find tips and ideas for making your revision more effective and maybe even more enjoyable. What follows gets your brain active, and active learning works!

Activity 1 – Stop and review

Step 1

When you have done no more than 5 minutes of revision reading STOP!

Step 2

Write a heading in your own words which sums up the topic you have been revising.

Step 3

Write a summary of what you have revised in no more than two sentences. Don't fool yourself by saying, "I know it, but I cannot put it into words". That just means you don't know it well enough. If you cannot write your summary, revise that section again, knowing that you must write a summary at the end of it. Many of you will have notebooks full of blue/black ink writing. Many of the pages will not be especially attractive or memorable so try to liven them up a bit with colour as you are reviewing and rewriting. **This is a great memory aid, and memory is the most important thing.**

Activity 2 — Use technology!

Why should everything be written down? Have you thought about "mental" maps, diagrams, cartoons and colour to help you learn? And rather than write down notes, why not record your revision material?

What about having a text message revision session with friends? Keep in touch with them to find out how and what they are revising and share ideas and questions.

Why not make a video diary where you tell the camera what you are doing, what you think you have learned and what you still have to do? No one has to see or hear it, but the process of having to organise your thoughts in a formal way to explain something is a very important learning practice.

Be sure to make use of electronic files. You could begin to summarise your class notes. Your typing might be slow, but it will get faster and the typed notes will be easier to read than the scribbles in your class notes. Try to add different fonts and colours to make your work stand out. You can easily Google relevant pictures, cartoons and diagrams which you can copy and paste to make your work more attractive and **MEMORABLE**.

Activity 3 – This is it. Do this and you will know lots!

Step 1

In this task you must be very honest with yourself! Find the SQA syllabus for your subject (www.sqa.org.uk). Look at how it is broken down into main topics called MANDATORY knowledge. That means stuff you MUST know.

Step 2

BEFORE you do ANY revision on this topic, write a list of everything that you already know about the subject. It might be quite a long list but you only need to write it once. It shows you all the information that is already in your long-term memory so you know what parts you do not need to revise!

Step 3

Pick a chapter or section from your book or revision notes. Choose a fairly large section or a whole chapter to get the most out of this activity.

With a buddy, use Skype, Facetime, Twitter or any other communication you have, to play the game "If this is the answer, what is the question?". For example, if you are revising Geography and the answer you provide is "meander", your buddy would have to make up a question like "What is the word that describes a feature of a river where it flows slowly and bends often from side to side?".

Make up 10 "answers" based on the content of the chapter or section you are using. Give this to your buddy to solve while you solve theirs.

Step 4

Construct a wordsearch of at least 10 X 10 squares. You can make it as big as you like but keep it realistic. Work together with a group of friends. Many apps allow you to make wordsearch puzzles online. The words and phrases can go in any direction and phrases can be split. Your puzzle must only contain facts linked to the topic you are revising. Your task is to find 10 bits of information to hide in your puzzle, but you must not repeat information that you used in Step 3. DO NOT show where the words are. Fill up empty squares with random letters. Remember to keep a note of where your answers are hidden but do not show your friends. When you have a complete puzzle, exchange it with a friend to solve each other's puzzle.

Step 5

Now make up 10 questions (not "answers" this time) based on the same chapter used in the previous two tasks. Again, you must find NEW information that you have not yet used. Now it's getting hard to find that new information! Again, give your questions to a friend to answer.

Step 6

As you have been doing the puzzles, your brain has been actively searching for new information. Now write a NEW LIST that contains only the new information you have discovered when doing the puzzles. Your new list is the one to look at repeatedly for short bursts over the next few days. Try to remember more and more of it without looking at it. After a few days, you should be able to add words from your second list to your first list as you increase the information in your long-term memory.

FINALLY! Be inspired...

Make a list of different revision ideas and beside each one write **THINGS I HAVE** tried, **THINGS I WILL** try and **THINGS I MIGHT** try. Don't be scared of trying something new.

And remember – "FAIL TO PREPARE AND PREPARE TO FAIL!"

Higher Mathematics

The course

The Higher course in Mathematics develops learners' mathematical rigour and the ability to use precise and concise mathematical language which assumes particular importance at this stage. Candidates who complete a Higher Mathematics course successfully are expected to have competence and confidence in applying mathematical techniques, manipulating symbolic expressions and communicating with mathematical correctness in the solution of problems.

The Higher qualification in Mathematics is designed to build upon and extend students' mathematical skills, knowledge and understanding in a way that recognises problem solving as an essential skill and enables them to integrate their knowledge of different aspects of the subject. You will acquire an enhanced awareness of the importance of mathematics to technology and to society in general. Where appropriate, mathematics will be developed in context and the use of mathematical techniques will be applied in social and vocational contexts related to likely progression routes such as commerce, engineering and science where the mathematics learned will be put to direct use.

The syllabus is designed to build upon your prior learning in the areas of algebra, geometry and trigonometry and to introduce you to elementary calculus.

How the course is graded

The grade you finally get for Higher Mathematics depends on two things:

- the internal assessments you do in school or college (the "NABs") – these don't count towards the final grade, but you must have passed them before you can achieve a final grade
- the examination consisting of two papers you sit in May – that's what this book is all about!

The examination

Paper 1 lasts 1 hour 30 minutes and there are 70 marks available in total. In this paper the use of a calculator is not permitted. There are two sections: section A consists of 20 objective test questions, each worth two marks, and section B is worth 30 marks. Section B contains a balance of short questions, designed to test knowledge and understanding, and extended response questions which also test problem solving skills.

Paper 2 lasts 1 hour 10 minutes and there are 60 marks available in total. In this paper, the use of a calculator is permitted. It too consists of short response questions, designed to test knowledge and understanding, as well as extended response questions which also test problem solving skills.

The SQA gives detailed advice in the Candidate Guidance Information section of the Higher Mathematics page on its website:
www.sqa.org.uk/sqa/39092.html.

Objective testing or multiple choice

An objective question offers you a choice of four answers. You have to choose the one you think is correct.

Answering the questions

These questions are answered on a special sheet. Each answer sheet contains spaces for providing the answer A, B, C or D for each question. If you decide the correct answer is given by A, you would record this by drawing a horizontal line with an **HB pencil** in box A.

Working

In the majority of questions you will need to do some working before making your choice.

Although this working will not be marked, it would be sensible to number the working and write neatly in case you need to go back and check it.

Method of marking

Each correct answer is worth 2 marks. Each incorrect answer is worth 0 marks. It is to your advantage to answer every objective question although you may not be absolutely sure of the correct answer. There is only one correct answer for each objective question. If you give two or more answers to any one question your answer will be marked as incorrect.

Types of Objective Questions

There are many different types of objective questions, but only the following types will be used in the Higher Mathematics examination.

1 Direct question
Example: You are given the equation of a curve and asked what the gradient of the tangent is at, say, the point where $x = 2$.

2 Direct question: options in a table
When there are two parts to an answer, the options may be listed in a table.

Example: You are given the equation of a graph with two unknowns, say p and q. You are then given two pieces of information, say the graph passes through the points (0, 1) and (1, 4), and you are asked for the values of p and q.

3 Direct instruction
Example: You are asked to find the integral of an expression and given four possible choices.

The majority of objective questions can be answered without any reference to the choices given by A, B, C or D. Occasionally however, you will come across a question which makes direct reference to the choices and quite often this will be a graphical question. .

Example: The diagram shows a sketch of the graph of $y = f(x)$. Which of the diagrams below is most likely to show a sketch of the graph of $y = 1 + f(x-3)$?

Preparation for the objective questions

To help you become familiar with the kind of questions you may be asked, you should practise specimen questions and you should time yourself, allowing about 40 to 45 minutes to complete a set of twenty. Work steadily through them and do not spend too long on any one question. There are 144 questions contained on the SQA website at www.sqa.uk/sqa/39134.html#announcement1 which can be used as practice.

Paper 1 Section B and Paper 2

Preparation and hints for the written response questions

You are encouraged to make connections between parts of questions, particularly where there are three or four sections to a question. These are almost always linked and, in some instances, an earlier result in part (a) or (b) is needed and its use would avoid further repeated work. Below are some key tips for your success.

Basic skills

You must practise your basic skills: expanding brackets; solving equations; manipulating algebraic expressions; and, in particular, working with exact values with trigonometric expressions and equations. These are essential skills for Higher Mathematics and should be practised throughout the duration of this course.

Communication

Communication is an important aspect of this examination and you are encouraged to show all working. This is particularly important in questions that contain the words "show that". In this type of question you must get to the result quoted in the question; failure to do so will usually prevent you gaining the final mark, at least for that question or part question. The work leading to the result must be shown fully for marks to be awarded. Looking at such questions and the corresponding marking instructions is invaluable.

Diagrams

Where a diagram is given on the question paper and you wish to annotate this, the diagram should be copied to your answer booklet first before any annotations are made. Do not miss essential working from your solutions: the question paper is not marked so annotations on it are lost.

Graph sketching

Graph sketching is an important and integral part of mathematics. Ensure that you take the opportunity to make sketches of graphs whenever possible throughout this course.

Make drawings

Try drawing what you visualise as the "picture", described within the wording of each, relevant question. This is a mathematical skill expected of most candidates at Higher level. Making a rough sketch of the diagram in your answer booklet may also help you to interpret the question and achieve more marks.

Marking instructions

Ensure that you look at the detailed marking instructions of past papers. They provide further advice and guidelines as well as showing you precisely where, and for what, marks are awarded.

Non-routine problems

When aiming for an A or B pass in Higher Mathematics it is important to be exposed to non-routine problems as often as possible throughout the course.

Notation

In all questions make sure that you use the correct notation. In particular, for integration questions, remember to include 'dx' within your integral.

Radians

Remember to work in radian measure when attempting any question involving both trigonometry and calculus.

Simplify

Get into the habit of simplifying expressions before doing any further work with them. This should make all subsequent work easier.

Subtraction

Be careful when subtracting one expression from another: ensure that any negative is applied correctly.

Good luck!

Remember that the rewards for passing Higher Mathematics are well worth it! Your pass will help you get the future you want for yourself. In the exam, be confident in your own ability. If you're not sure how to answer a question, trust your instincts and just give it a go anyway – keep calm and don't panic! GOOD LUCK!

HIGHER

2010

[BLANK PAGE]

X100/301

NATIONAL	FRIDAY, 21 MAY	**MATHEMATICS**
QUALIFICATIONS	9.00 AM – 10.30 AM	HIGHER
2010		Paper 1
		(Non-calculator)

Read carefully

Calculators may <u>NOT</u> be used in this paper.

Section A – Questions 1–20 (40 marks)

Instructions for completion of **Section A** are given on page two.

For this section of the examination you must use an **HB pencil**.

Section B (30 marks)

1   Full credit will be given only where the solution contains appropriate working.

2   Answers obtained by readings from scale drawings will not receive any credit.

Read carefully

1 Check that the answer sheet provided is for **Mathematics Higher (Section A)**.

2 For this section of the examination you must use an **HB pencil** and, where necessary, an eraser.

3 Check that the answer sheet you have been given has **your name**, **date of birth**, **SCN** (Scottish Candidate Number) and **Centre Name** printed on it.

Do not change any of these details.

4 If any of this information is wrong, tell the Invigilator immediately.

5 If this information is correct, **print** your name and seat number in the boxes provided.

6 The answer to each question is **either** A, B, C or D. Decide what your answer is, then, using your pencil, put a horizontal line in the space provided (see sample question below).

7 There is **only one correct** answer to each question.

8 Rough working should **not** be done on your answer sheet.

9 At the end of the exam, put the **answer sheet for Section A inside the front cover of your answer book**.

Sample Question

A curve has equation $y = x^3 - 4x$.

What is the gradient at the point where $x = 2$?

   A 8

   B 1

   C 0

   D −4

The correct answer is **A**—8. The answer **A** has been clearly marked in **pencil** with a horizontal line (see below).

Changing an answer

If you decide to change your answer, carefully erase your first answer and, using your pencil, fill in the answer you want. The answer below has been changed to **D**.

A B C D

FORMULAE LIST

Circle:

The equation $x^2 + y^2 + 2gx + 2fy + c = 0$ represents a circle centre $(-g, -f)$ and radius $\sqrt{g^2 + f^2 - c}$.

The equation $(x - a)^2 + (y - b)^2 = r^2$ represents a circle centre (a, b) and radius r.

Scalar Product: $\mathbf{a}.\mathbf{b} = |\mathbf{a}|\,|\mathbf{b}|\cos\theta$, where θ is the angle between $\mathbf{a}$ and $\mathbf{b}$

or $\mathbf{a}.\mathbf{b} = a_1 b_1 + a_2 b_2 + a_3 b_3$ where $\mathbf{a} = \begin{pmatrix} a_1 \\ a_2 \\ a_3 \end{pmatrix}$ and $\mathbf{b} = \begin{pmatrix} b_1 \\ b_2 \\ b_3 \end{pmatrix}$.

Trigonometric formulae:
$$\sin(A \pm B) = \sin A \cos B \pm \cos A \sin B$$
$$\cos(A \pm B) = \cos A \cos B \mp \sin A \sin B$$
$$\sin 2A = 2\sin A \cos A$$
$$\cos 2A = \cos^2 A - \sin^2 A$$
$$= 2\cos^2 A - 1$$
$$= 1 - 2\sin^2 A$$

Table of standard derivatives:

$f(x)$	$f'(x)$
$\sin ax$	$a\cos ax$
$\cos ax$	$-a\sin ax$

Table of standard integrals:

$f(x)$	$\int f(x)\,dx$
$\sin ax$	$-\dfrac{1}{a}\cos ax + C$
$\cos ax$	$\dfrac{1}{a}\sin ax + C$

[Turn over

SECTION A

ALL questions should be attempted.

1. A line L is perpendicular to the line with equation $2x - 3y - 6 = 0$.

    What is the gradient of the line L?

    A $-\dfrac{3}{2}$

    B $-\dfrac{1}{2}$

    C $\dfrac{2}{3}$

    D   2

2. A sequence is defined by the recurrence relation $u_{n+1} = 2u_n + 3$ and $u_0 = 1$.

    What is the value of u_2?

    A   7

    B   10

    C   13

    D   16

3. Given that $\mathbf{u} = \begin{pmatrix} 2 \\ 0 \\ 1 \end{pmatrix}$ and $\mathbf{v} = \begin{pmatrix} -1 \\ 2 \\ 4 \end{pmatrix}$, find $3\mathbf{u} - 2\mathbf{v}$ in component form.

    A $\begin{pmatrix} 4 \\ -1 \\ -5 \end{pmatrix}$

    B $\begin{pmatrix} 4 \\ -4 \\ 11 \end{pmatrix}$

    C $\begin{pmatrix} 8 \\ -1 \\ 5 \end{pmatrix}$

    D $\begin{pmatrix} 8 \\ -4 \\ -5 \end{pmatrix}$

4. The diagram shows the graph with equation of the form $y = a\cos bx$ for $0 \le x \le 2\pi$.

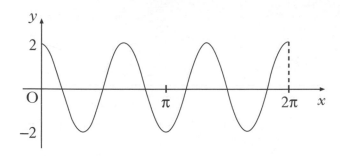

What is the equation of this graph?

A $y = 2\cos 3x$

B $y = 2\cos 2x$

C $y = 3\cos 2x$

D $y = 4\cos 3x$

5. When $x^2 + 8x + 3$ is written in the form $(x + p)^2 + q$, what is the value of q?

A -19

B -13

C -5

D 19

[Turn over

6. The roots of the equation $kx^2 - 3x + 2 = 0$ are equal.

What is the value of k?

   A $-\dfrac{9}{8}$

   B $-\dfrac{8}{9}$

   C $\dfrac{8}{9}$

   D $\dfrac{9}{8}$

7. A sequence is generated by the recurrence relation $u_{n+1} = \dfrac{1}{4}u_n + 7$, with $u_0 = -2$.

What is the limit of this sequence as $n \to \infty$?

   A $\dfrac{1}{28}$

   B $\dfrac{28}{5}$

   C $\dfrac{28}{3}$

   D 28

8. The equation of the circle shown in the diagram is $x^2 + y^2 - 6x - 10y + 9 = 0$.

The x-axis and the line l are parallel tangents to the circle.

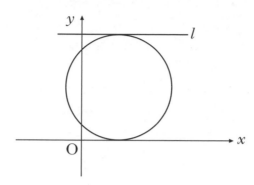

What is the equation of line l?

A　$y = 5$

B　$y = 10$

C　$y = 18$

D　$y = 20$

9. Find $\int (2x^{-4} + \cos 5x)\, dx$.

A　$-\dfrac{2}{5}x^{-5} - 5\sin 5x + c$

B　$-\dfrac{2}{5}x^{-5} + \dfrac{1}{5}\sin 5x + c$

C　$-\dfrac{2}{3}x^{-3} + \dfrac{1}{5}\sin 5x + c$

D　$-\dfrac{2}{3}x^{-3} - 5\sin 5x + c$

10. The vectors $x\mathbf{i} + 5\mathbf{j} + 7\mathbf{k}$ and $-3\mathbf{i} + 2\mathbf{j} - \mathbf{k}$ are perpendicular.

What is the value of x?

A　0

B　1

C　$\dfrac{4}{3}$

D　$\dfrac{10}{3}$

[Turn over

11. Functions f and g are defined on suitable domains by $f(x) = \cos x$ and $g(x) = x + \dfrac{\pi}{6}$.

What is the value of $f\left(g\left(\dfrac{\pi}{6}\right)\right)$?

A $\dfrac{1}{2} + \dfrac{\pi}{6}$

B $\dfrac{\sqrt{3}}{2} + \dfrac{\pi}{6}$

C $\dfrac{\sqrt{3}}{2}$

D $\dfrac{1}{2}$

12. If $f(x) = \dfrac{1}{\sqrt[5]{x}}$, $x \neq 0$, what is $f'(x)$?

A $-\dfrac{1}{5}x^{-\frac{6}{5}}$

B $-\dfrac{1}{5}x^{-\frac{4}{5}}$

C $-\dfrac{5}{2}x^{-\frac{7}{2}}$

D $-\dfrac{5}{2}x^{-\frac{3}{2}}$

Marks

SECTION B

ALL questions should be attempted.

21. Triangle ABC has vertices A(4, 0), B(−4, 16) and C(18, 20), as shown in the diagram opposite.

Medians AP and CR intersect at the point T(6, 12).

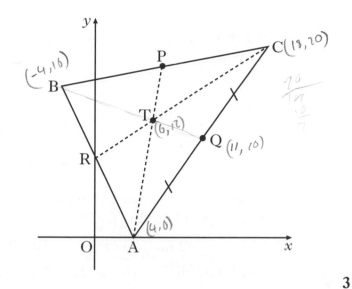

(a) Find the equation of median BQ.   **3**

(b) Verify that T lies on BQ.   **1**

(c) Find the ratio in which T divides BQ.   **2**

22. (a) (i) Show that $(x - 1)$ is a factor of $f(x) = 2x^3 + x^2 - 8x + 5$.

(ii) Hence factorise $f(x)$ fully.   **5**

(b) Solve $2x^3 + x^2 - 8x + 5 = 0$.   **1**

(c) The line with equation $y = 2x - 3$ is a tangent to the curve with equation $y = 2x^3 + x^2 - 6x + 2$ at the point G.

Find the coordinates of G.   **5**

(d) This tangent meets the curve again at the point H.

Write down the coordinates of H.   **1**

[Turn over for Question 23 on *Page fourteen*

Marks

23. (*a*) Diagram 1 shows a right angled triangle, where the line OA has equation $3x - 2y = 0$.

    (i) Show that $\tan a = \dfrac{3}{2}$.

    (ii) Find the value of $\sin a$.

4

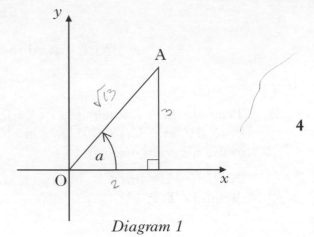

Diagram 1

(*b*) A second right angled triangle is added as shown in Diagram 2.

The line OB has equation $3x - 4y = 0$.

Find the values of $\sin b$ and $\cos b$.

4

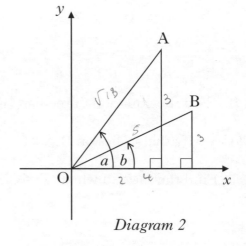

Diagram 2

(*c*) (i) Find the value of $\sin(a - b)$.

    (ii) State the value of $\sin(b - a)$.

4

[END OF SECTION B]

[END OF QUESTION PAPER]

X100/302

NATIONAL
QUALIFICATIONS
2010

FRIDAY, 21 MAY
10.50 AM – 12.00 NOON

MATHEMATICS
HIGHER
Paper 2

Read Carefully

1 **Calculators may be used in this paper.**

2 Full credit will be given only where the solution contains appropriate working.

3 Answers obtained by readings from scale drawings will not receive any credit.

LI X100/302 6/31310

FORMULAE LIST

Circle:

The equation $x^2 + y^2 + 2gx + 2fy + c = 0$ represents a circle centre $(-g, -f)$ and radius $\sqrt{g^2 + f^2 - c}$.

The equation $(x - a)^2 + (y - b)^2 = r^2$ represents a circle centre (a, b) and radius r.

Scalar Product: $\mathbf{a} . \mathbf{b} = |\mathbf{a}|\,|\mathbf{b}| \cos \theta$, where θ is the angle between $\mathbf{a}$ and $\mathbf{b}$

or $\mathbf{a} . \mathbf{b} = a_1 b_1 + a_2 b_2 + a_3 b_3$ where $\mathbf{a} = \begin{pmatrix} a_1 \\ a_2 \\ a_3 \end{pmatrix}$ and $\mathbf{b} = \begin{pmatrix} b_1 \\ b_2 \\ b_3 \end{pmatrix}$.

Trigonometric formulae: $\sin (A \pm B) = \sin A \cos B \pm \cos A \sin B$

$\cos (A \pm B) = \cos A \cos B \mp \sin A \sin B$

$\sin 2A = 2\sin A \cos A$

$\cos 2A = \cos^2 A - \sin^2 A$

$= 2\cos^2 A - 1$

$= 1 - 2\sin^2 A$

Table of standard derivatives:

$f(x)$	$f'(x)$
$\sin ax$	$a \cos ax$
$\cos ax$	$-a \sin ax$

Table of standard integrals:

$f(x)$	$\int f(x)\,dx$
$\sin ax$	$-\dfrac{1}{a} \cos ax + C$
$\cos ax$	$\dfrac{1}{a} \sin ax + C$

Marks

ALL questions should be attempted.

1. The diagram shows a cuboid OPQR, STUV relative to the coordinate axes.

    P is the point (4, 0, 0),
    Q is (4, 2, 0) and U is (4, 2, 3).

    M is the midpoint of OR.

    N is the point on UQ such that
    $UN = \frac{1}{3}UQ$.

    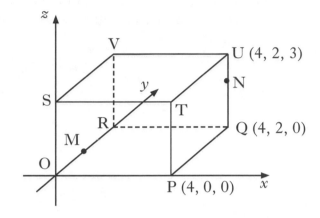

    (a) State the coordinates of M and N.   2

    (b) Express $\overrightarrow{VM}$ and $\overrightarrow{VN}$ in component form. 2

    (c) Calculate the size of angle MVN.   5

2. (a) $12 \cos x° - 5 \sin x°$ can be expressed in the form $k \cos(x + a)°$, where $k > 0$ and $0 \le a < 360$.

    Calculate the values of k and a.   4

    (b) (i) Hence state the maximum and minimum values of $12 \cos x° - 5 \sin x°$.

    (ii) Determine the values of x, in the interval $0 \le x < 360$, at which these maximum and minimum values occur.   3

    [Turn over

Marks

3. (a) (i) Show that the line with equation $y = 3 - x$ is a tangent to the circle with equation $x^2 + y^2 + 14x + 4y - 19 = 0$.

   (ii) Find the coordinates of the point of contact, P.   **5**

   (b) Relative to a suitable set of coordinate axes, the diagram below shows the circle from (a) and a second smaller circle with centre C.

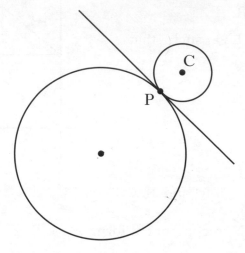

   The line $y = 3 - x$ is a common tangent at the point P.

   The radius of the larger circle is three times the radius of the smaller circle.

   Find the equation of the smaller circle.   **6**

4. Solve $2\cos 2x - 5\cos x - 4 = 0$ for $0 \le x < 2\pi$.   **5**

Marks

5. The parabolas with equations $y = 10 - x^2$ and $y = \frac{2}{5}(10 - x^2)$ are shown in the diagram below.

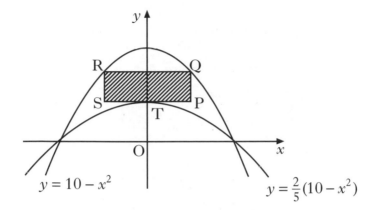

A rectangle PQRS is placed between the two parabolas as shown, so that:

- Q and R lie on the upper parabola;
- RQ and SP are parallel to the x-axis;
- T, the turning point of the lower parabola, lies on SP.

(a) (i) If TP = x units, find an expression for the length of PQ.

   (ii) Hence show that the area, A, of rectangle PQRS is given by

$$A(x) = 12x - 2x^3.$$

3

(b) Find the maximum area of this rectangle.

6

[Turn over for Questions 6 and 7 on *Page six*

Marks

6. (a) A curve has equation $y = (2x - 9)^{\frac{1}{2}}$.

   Show that the equation of the tangent to this curve at the point where $x = 9$ is $y = \frac{1}{3}x$.   **5**

   (b) Diagram 1 shows part of the curve and the tangent.

   The curve cuts the x-axis at the point A.

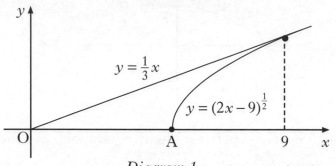

Diagram 1

   Find the coordinates of point A.   **1**

   (c) Calculate the shaded area shown in diagram 2.   **7**

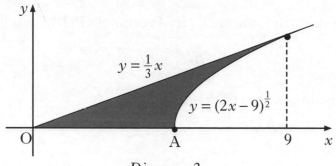

Diagram 2

7. (a) Given that $\log_4 x = P$, show that $\log_{16} x = \frac{1}{2}P$.   **3**

   (b) Solve $\log_3 x + \log_9 x = 12$.   **3**

[*END OF QUESTION PAPER*]

[BLANK PAGE]

X100/301

| NATIONAL QUALIFICATIONS 2011 | WEDNESDAY, 18 MAY 9.00 AM – 10.30 AM | MATHEMATICS HIGHER Paper 1 (Non-calculator) |

Read carefully

Calculators may <u>NOT</u> be used in this paper.

Section A – Questions 1–20 (40 marks)

Instructions for completion of **Section A** are given on page two.

For this section of the examination you must use an **HB pencil**.

Section B (30 marks)

1   Full credit will be given only where the solution contains appropriate working.

2   Answers obtained by readings from scale drawings will not receive any credit.

Read carefully

1 Check that the answer sheet provided is for **Mathematics Higher (Section A)**.

2 For this section of the examination you must use an **HB pencil** and, where necessary, an eraser.

3 Check that the answer sheet you have been given has **your name**, **date of birth**, **SCN** (Scottish Candidate Number) and **Centre Name** printed on it.

   Do not change any of these details.

4 If any of this information is wrong, tell the Invigilator immediately.

5 If this information is correct, **print** your name and seat number in the boxes provided.

6 The answer to each question is **either** A, B, C or D. Decide what your answer is, then, using your pencil, put a horizontal line in the space provided (see sample question below).

7 There is **only one correct** answer to each question.

8 Rough working should **not** be done on your answer sheet.

9 At the end of the exam, put the **answer sheet for Section A inside the front cover of your answer book**.

Sample Question

A curve has equation $y = x^3 - 4x$.

What is the gradient at the point where $x = 2$?

   A 8

   B 1

   C 0

   D −4

The correct answer is **A—8**. The answer **A** has been clearly marked in **pencil** with a horizontal line (see below).

Changing an answer

If you decide to change your answer, carefully erase your first answer and, using your pencil, fill in the answer you want. The answer below has been changed to **D**.

FORMULAE LIST

Circle:

The equation $x^2 + y^2 + 2gx + 2fy + c = 0$ represents a circle centre $(-g, -f)$ and radius $\sqrt{g^2 + f^2 - c}$.

The equation $(x - a)^2 + (y - b)^2 = r^2$ represents a circle centre (a, b) and radius r.

Scalar Product: $\mathbf{a}.\mathbf{b} = |\mathbf{a}|\,|\mathbf{b}|\cos\theta$, where θ is the angle between $\mathbf{a}$ and $\mathbf{b}$

or $\mathbf{a}.\mathbf{b} = a_1b_1 + a_2b_2 + a_3b_3$ where $\mathbf{a} = \begin{pmatrix} a_1 \\ a_2 \\ a_3 \end{pmatrix}$ and $\mathbf{b} = \begin{pmatrix} b_1 \\ b_2 \\ b_3 \end{pmatrix}$.

Trigonometric formulae:

$$\sin(A \pm B) = \sin A \cos B \pm \cos A \sin B$$
$$\cos(A \pm B) = \cos A \cos B \mp \sin A \sin B$$
$$\sin 2A = 2\sin A \cos A$$
$$\cos 2A = \cos^2 A - \sin^2 A$$
$$= 2\cos^2 A - 1$$
$$= 1 - 2\sin^2 A$$

Table of standard derivatives:

$f(x)$	$f'(x)$
$\sin ax$	$a\cos ax$
$\cos ax$	$-a\sin ax$

Table of standard integrals:

$f(x)$	$\int f(x)\,dx$
$\sin ax$	$-\dfrac{1}{a}\cos ax + C$
$\cos ax$	$\dfrac{1}{a}\sin ax + C$

[Turn over

SECTION A

ALL questions should be attempted.

1. Given that $\mathbf{p} = \begin{pmatrix} 2 \\ 5 \\ -7 \end{pmatrix}$, $\mathbf{q} = \begin{pmatrix} 1 \\ 0 \\ -1 \end{pmatrix}$ and $\mathbf{r} = \begin{pmatrix} -4 \\ 2 \\ 0 \end{pmatrix}$, express $2\mathbf{p} - \mathbf{q} - \frac{1}{2}\mathbf{r}$ in component form.

   A $\begin{pmatrix} 1 \\ 9 \\ -15 \end{pmatrix}$

   B $\begin{pmatrix} 1 \\ 11 \\ -13 \end{pmatrix}$

   C $\begin{pmatrix} 5 \\ 9 \\ -13 \end{pmatrix}$

   D $\begin{pmatrix} 5 \\ 11 \\ -15 \end{pmatrix}$

2. A line l has equation $3y + 2x = 6$.

   What is the gradient of any line parallel to l?

   A -2

   B $-\dfrac{2}{3}$

   C $\dfrac{3}{2}$

   D 2

3. The diagram shows the graph of $y = f(x)$.

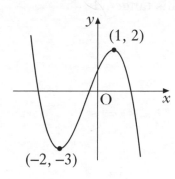

Which of the following shows the graph of $y = f(x + 2) - 1$?

A

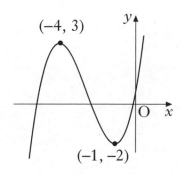

B

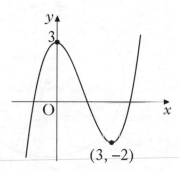

C

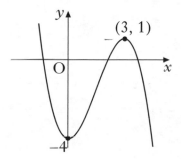

D

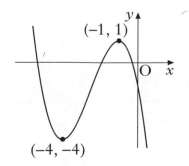

[Turn over

4. A tangent to the curve with equation $y = x^3 - 2x$ is drawn at the point (2, 4).

   What is the gradient of this tangent?

   A   2

   B   3

   C   4

   D   10

5. If $x^2 - 8x + 7$ is written in the form $(x - p)^2 + q$, what is the value of q?

   A   −9

   B   −1

   C   7

   D   23

6. The point P(2, −3) lies on the circle with centre C as shown.

   The gradient of CP is −2.

   What is the equation of the tangent at P?

   A $y + 3 = -2(x - 2)$

   B $y - 3 = -2(x + 2)$

   C $y + 3 = \frac{1}{2}(x - 2)$

   D $y - 3 = \frac{1}{2}(x + 2)$

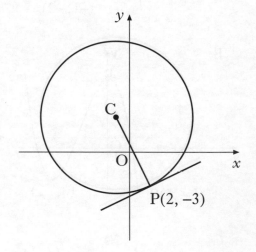

7. A function f is defined on the set of real numbers by $f(x) = x^3 - x^2 + x + 3$.

   What is the remainder when $f(x)$ is divided by $(x - 1)$?

   A   0

   B   2

   C   3

   D   4

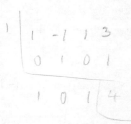

8. A line makes an angle of 30° with the positive direction of the x-axis as shown.

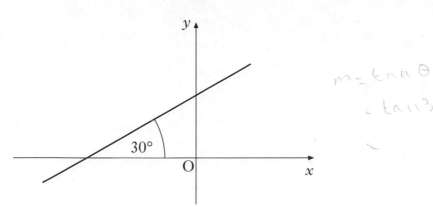

What is the gradient of the line?

A $\dfrac{1}{\sqrt{3}}$

B $\dfrac{1}{\sqrt{2}}$

C $\dfrac{1}{2}$

D $\dfrac{\sqrt{3}}{2}$

9. The discriminant of a quadratic equation is 23.

Here are two statements about this quadratic equation:

(1) the roots are real;

(2) the roots are rational.

Which of the following is true?

A   Neither statement is correct.

B   Only statement (1) is correct.

C   Only statement (2) is correct.

D   Both statements are correct.

[Turn over

10. Solve $2\cos x = \sqrt{3}$ for x, where $0 \leq x < 2\pi$.

A $\quad \dfrac{\pi}{3}$ and $\dfrac{5\pi}{3}$

B $\quad \dfrac{\pi}{3}$ and $\dfrac{2\pi}{3}$

C $\quad \dfrac{\pi}{6}$ and $\dfrac{5\pi}{6}$

D $\quad \dfrac{\pi}{6}$ and $\dfrac{11\pi}{6}$

11. Find $\displaystyle\int \left(4x^{\frac{1}{2}} + x^{-3} \right) dx$, where $x > 0$.

A $\quad 2x^{-\frac{1}{2}} - 3x^{-4} + c$

B $\quad 2x^{-\frac{1}{2}} - \dfrac{1}{2}x^{-2} + c$

C $\quad \dfrac{8}{3}x^{\frac{3}{2}} - 3x^{-4} + c$

D $\quad \dfrac{8}{3}x^{\frac{3}{2}} - \dfrac{1}{2}x^{-2} + c$

12. The diagram shows two right-angled triangles with sides and angles as given.

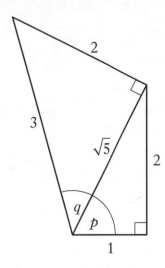

What is the value of $\sin(p + q)$?

A $\dfrac{2}{\sqrt{5}} + \dfrac{2}{3}$

B $\dfrac{2}{\sqrt{5}} + \dfrac{\sqrt{5}}{3}$

C $\dfrac{2}{3} + \dfrac{2}{3\sqrt{5}}$

D $\dfrac{4}{3\sqrt{5}} + \dfrac{1}{3}$

13. Given that $f(x) = 4\sin 3x$, find $f'(0)$.

A   0

B   1

C   12

D   36

[Turn over

14. An equilateral triangle of side 3 units is shown.

The vectors **p** and **q** are as represented in the diagram.

What is the value of **p**.**q**?

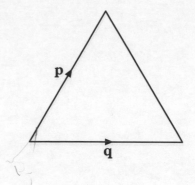

A   9

B $\dfrac{9}{2}$

C $\dfrac{9}{\sqrt{2}}$

D   0

15. Given that the points S(−4, 5, 1), T(−16, −4, 16) and U(−24, −10, 26) are collinear, calculate the ratio in which T divides SU.

A   2 : 3

B   3 : 2

C   2 : 5

D   3 : 5

16. Find $\displaystyle\int \dfrac{1}{3x^4}\,dx$, where $x \neq 0$.

A $-\dfrac{1}{9x^3}+c$

B $-\dfrac{1}{x^3}+c$

C $\dfrac{1}{x^3}+c$

D $\dfrac{1}{12x^3}+c$

17. The diagram shows the graph of a cubic.

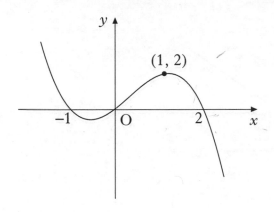

What is the equation of this cubic?

A $y = -x(x + 1)(x - 2)$

B $y = -x(x - 1)(x + 2)$

C $y = x(x + 1)(x - 2)$

D $y = x(x - 1)(x + 2)$

18. If $f(x) = (x - 3)(x + 5)$, for what values of x is the graph of $y = f(x)$ above the x-axis?

A $-5 < x < 3$

B $-3 < x < 5$

C $x < -5, x > 3$

D $x < -3, x > 5$

[Turn over

19. Which of the following diagrams represents the graph with equation $\log_3 y = x$?

A
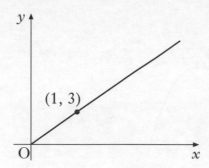

B
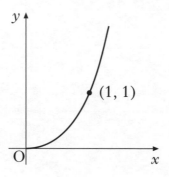

C
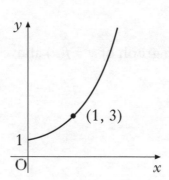

D
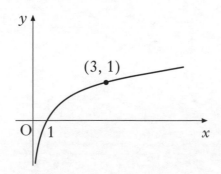

20. On a suitable domain, D, a function g is defined by $g(x) = \sin^2 \sqrt{x-2}$.

Which of the following gives the real values of x in D and the corresponding values of $g(x)$?

A $x \geq 0$ and $-1 \leq g(x) \leq 1$

B $x \geq 0$ and $0 \leq g(x) \leq 1$

C $x \geq 2$ and $-1 \leq g(x) \leq 1$

D $x \geq 2$ and $0 \leq g(x) \leq 1$

[END OF SECTION A]

[Turn over for SECTION B

Marks

SECTION B

ALL questions should be attempted.

21. A quadrilateral has vertices A(–1, 8), B(7, 12), C(8, 5) and D(2, –3) as shown in the diagram.

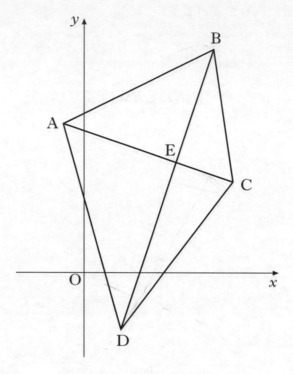

(a) Find the equation of diagonal BD.   2

(b) The equation of diagonal AC is $x + 3y = 23$.

Find the coordinates of E, the point of intersection of the diagonals.   3

(c) (i) Find the equation of the perpendicular bisector of AB.

(ii) Show that this line passes through E.   5

Marks

22. A function f is defined on the set of real numbers by $f(x) = (x - 2)(x^2 + 1)$.

(a) Find where the graph of $y = f(x)$ cuts:

   (i) the x-axis;

   (ii) the y-axis.   **2**

(b) Find the coordinates of the stationary points on the curve with equation $y = f(x)$ and determine their nature.   **8**

(c) On separate diagrams sketch the graphs of:

   (i) $y = f(x)$;

   (ii) $y = -f(x)$.   **3**

23. (a) Solve $\cos 2x° - 3\cos x° + 2 = 0$ for $0 \le x < 360$.   **5**

(b) Hence solve $\cos 4x° - 3\cos 2x° + 2 = 0$ for $0 \le x < 360$.   **2**

[END OF SECTION B]

[END OF QUESTION PAPER]

[BLANK PAGE]

X100/302

NATIONAL
QUALIFICATIONS
2011

WEDNESDAY, 18 MAY
10.50 AM – 12.00 NOON

MATHEMATICS
HIGHER
Paper 2

Read Carefully

1　**Calculators may be used in this paper.**

2　Full credit will be given only where the solution contains appropriate working.

3　Answers obtained by readings from scale drawings will not receive any credit.

FORMULAE LIST

Circle:

The equation $x^2 + y^2 + 2gx + 2fy + c = 0$ represents a circle centre $(-g, -f)$ and radius $\sqrt{g^2 + f^2 - c}$.

The equation $(x - a)^2 + (y - b)^2 = r^2$ represents a circle centre (a, b) and radius r.

Scalar Product: $\mathbf{a}.\mathbf{b} = |\mathbf{a}|\,|\mathbf{b}| \cos \theta$, where θ is the angle between $\mathbf{a}$ and $\mathbf{b}$

or $\mathbf{a}.\mathbf{b} = a_1 b_1 + a_2 b_2 + a_3 b_3$ where $\mathbf{a} = \begin{pmatrix} a_1 \\ a_2 \\ a_3 \end{pmatrix}$ and $\mathbf{b} = \begin{pmatrix} b_1 \\ b_2 \\ b_3 \end{pmatrix}$.

Trigonometric formulae:
$$\sin (A \pm B) = \sin A \cos B \pm \cos A \sin B$$
$$\cos (A \pm B) = \cos A \cos B \mp \sin A \sin B$$
$$\sin 2A = 2\sin A \cos A$$
$$\cos 2A = \cos^2 A - \sin^2 A$$
$$= 2\cos^2 A - 1$$
$$= 1 - 2\sin^2 A$$

Table of standard derivatives:

$f(x)$	$f'(x)$
$\sin ax$	$a \cos ax$
$\cos ax$	$-a \sin ax$

Table of standard integrals:

$f(x)$	$\int f(x)\,dx$
$\sin ax$	$-\dfrac{1}{a} \cos ax + C$
$\cos ax$	$\dfrac{1}{a} \sin ax + C$

Marks

ALL questions should be attempted.

1. D,OABC is a square based pyramid as shown in the diagram below.

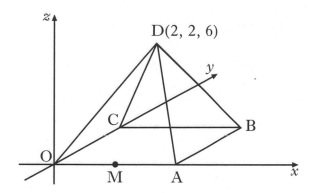

O is the origin, D is the point (2, 2, 6) and OA = 4 units.

M is the mid-point of OA.

(a) State the coordinates of B. **1**

(b) Express $\overrightarrow{DB}$ and $\overrightarrow{DM}$ in component form. **3**

(c) Find the size of angle BDM. **5**

2. Functions f, g and h are defined on the set of real numbers by

- $f(x) = x^3 - 1$
- $g(x) = 3x + 1$
- $h(x) = 4x - 5$.

(a) Find $g(f(x))$. **2**

(b) Show that $g(f(x)) + xh(x) = 3x^3 + 4x^2 - 5x - 2$. **1**

(c) (i) Show that $(x - 1)$ is a factor of $3x^3 + 4x^2 - 5x - 2$.

(ii) Factorise $3x^3 + 4x^2 - 5x - 2$ fully. **5**

(d) Hence solve $g(f(x)) + xh(x) = 0$. **1**

[Turn over

Marks

3. (a) A sequence is defined by $u_{n+1} = -\frac{1}{2}u_n$ with $u_0 = -16$.

Write down the values of u_1 and u_2.

1

(b) A second sequence is given by 4, 5, 7, 11, ...

It is generated by the recurrence relation $v_{n+1} = pv_n + q$ with $v_1 = 4$.

Find the values of p and q.

3

(c) Either the sequence in (a) or the sequence in (b) has a limit.

(i) Calculate this limit.

(ii) Why does the other sequence not have a limit?

3

4. The diagram shows the curve with equation $y = x^3 - x^2 - 4x + 4$ and the line with equation $y = 2x + 4$.

The curve and the line intersect at the points $(-2, 0)$, $(0, 4)$ and $(3, 10)$.

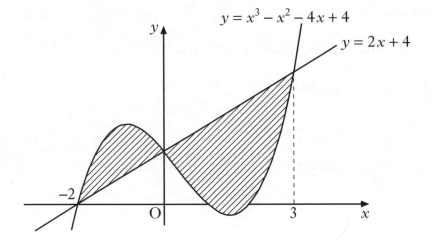

Calculate the total shaded area.

10

Marks

5. Variables x and y are related by the equation $y = kx^n$.

   The graph of $\log_2 y$ against $\log_2 x$ is a straight line through the points $(0, 5)$ and $(4, 7)$, as shown in the diagram.

   Find the values of k and n.

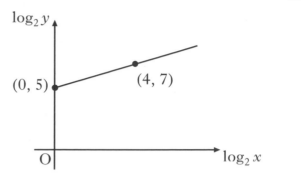

5

6. (a) The expression $3\sin x - 5\cos x$ can be written in the form $R\sin(x+a)$ where $R > 0$ and $0 \le a < 2\pi$.

   Calculate the values of R and a.

4

   (b) Hence find the value of t, where $0 \le t \le 2$, for which

   $$\int_0^t (3\cos x + 5\sin x)\, dx = 3.$$

7

7. Circle C_1 has equation $(x + 1)^2 + (y - 1)^2 = 121$.

   A circle C_2 with equation $x^2 + y^2 - 4x + 6y + p = 0$ is drawn inside C_1.

   The circles have no points of contact.

   What is the range of values of p?

9

[END OF QUESTION PAPER]

[BLANK PAGE]

HIGHER

2012

[BLANK PAGE]

X100/12/02

NATIONAL QUALIFICATIONS 2012	MONDAY, 21 MAY 1.00 PM – 2.30 PM	**MATHEMATICS HIGHER** Paper 1 (Non-calculator)

Read carefully

Calculators may <u>NOT</u> be used in this paper.

Section A – Questions 1–20 (40 marks)

Instructions for completion of **Section A** are given on Page two.

For this section of the examination you must use an **HB pencil**.

Section B (30 marks)

1   Full credit will be given only where the solution contains appropriate working.

2   Answers obtained by readings from scale drawings will not receive any credit.

Read carefully

1 Check that the answer sheet provided is for **Mathematics Higher (Section A)**.

2 For this section of the examination you must use an **HB pencil** and, where necessary, an eraser.

3 Check that the answer sheet you have been given has **your name**, **date of birth**, **SCN** (Scottish Candidate Number) and **Centre Name** printed on it.

   Do not change any of these details.

4 If any of this information is wrong, tell the Invigilator immediately.

5 If this information is correct, **print** your name and seat number in the boxes provided.

6 The answer to each question is **either** A, B, C or D. Decide what your answer is, then, using your pencil, put a horizontal line in the space provided (see sample question below).

7 There is **only one correct** answer to each question.

8 Rough working should **not** be done on your answer sheet.

9 At the end of the exam, put the **answer sheet for Section A inside the front cover of your answer book**.

Sample Question

A curve has equation $y = x^3 - 4x$.

What is the gradient at the point where $x = 2$?

   A   8

   B   1

   C   0

   D -4

The correct answer is **A**—8. The answer **A** has been clearly marked in **pencil** with a horizontal line (see below).

Changing an answer

If you decide to change your answer, carefully erase your first answer and, using your pencil, fill in the answer you want. The answer below has been changed to **D**.

A   B   C   D

FORMULAE LIST

Circle:

The equation $x^2 + y^2 + 2gx + 2fy + c = 0$ represents a circle centre $(-g, -f)$ and radius $\sqrt{g^2 + f^2 - c}$.

The equation $(x - a)^2 + (y - b)^2 = r^2$ represents a circle centre (a, b) and radius r.

Scalar Product: $\mathbf{a.b} = |\mathbf{a}||\mathbf{b}| \cos \theta$, where θ is the angle between $\mathbf{a}$ and $\mathbf{b}$

or $\mathbf{a.b} = a_1b_1 + a_2b_2 + a_3b_3$ where $\mathbf{a} = \begin{pmatrix} a_1 \\ a_2 \\ a_3 \end{pmatrix}$ and $\mathbf{b} = \begin{pmatrix} b_1 \\ b_2 \\ b_3 \end{pmatrix}$.

Trigonometric formulae:
$$\sin (A \pm B) = \sin A \cos B \pm \cos A \sin B$$
$$\cos (A \pm B) = \cos A \cos B \mp \sin A \sin B$$
$$\sin 2A = 2\sin A \cos A$$
$$\cos 2A = \cos^2 A - \sin^2 A$$
$$= 2\cos^2 A - 1$$
$$= 1 - 2\sin^2 A$$

Table of standard derivatives:

$f(x)$	$f'(x)$
$\sin ax$	$a \cos ax$
$\cos ax$	$-a \sin ax$

Table of standard integrals:

$f(x)$	$\int f(x)dx$
$\sin ax$	$-\dfrac{1}{a} \cos ax + C$
$\cos ax$	$\dfrac{1}{a} \sin ax + C$

[Turn over

SECTION A

ALL questions should be attempted.

1. A sequence is defined by the recurrence relation $u_{n+1} = 3u_n + 4$, with $u_0 = 1$.

   Find the value of u_2.

   A   7

   B   10

   C   25

   D   35

2. What is the gradient of the tangent to the curve with equation $y = x^3 - 6x + 1$ at the point where $x = -2$?

   A   −24

   B   3

   C   5

   D   6

3. If $x^2 - 6x + 14$ is written in the form $(x - p)^2 + q$, what is the value of q?

   A   −22

   B   5

   C   14

   D   50

4. What is the gradient of the line shown in the diagram?

   A $-\sqrt{3}$

   B $-\dfrac{1}{\sqrt{3}}$

   C $-\dfrac{1}{2}$

   D $-\dfrac{\sqrt{3}}{2}$

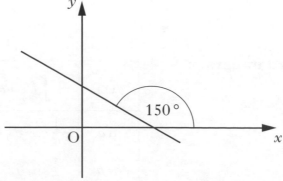

5. The diagram shows a right-angled triangle with sides and angles as marked.

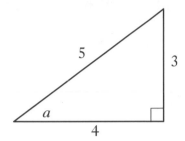

What is the value of $\cos 2a$?

A $\quad \dfrac{7}{25}$

B $\quad \dfrac{3}{5}$

C $\quad \dfrac{24}{25}$

D $\quad \dfrac{6}{5}$

6. If $y = 3x^{-2} + 2x^{\frac{3}{2}}$, $x > 0$, determine $\dfrac{dy}{dx}$.

A $\quad -6x^{-3} + \dfrac{4}{5}x^{\frac{5}{2}}$

B $\quad -3x^{-1} + 3x^{\frac{1}{2}}$

C $\quad -6x^{-3} + 3x^{\frac{1}{2}}$

D $\quad -3x^{-1} + \dfrac{4}{5}x^{\frac{5}{2}}$

7. If $\mathbf{u} = \begin{pmatrix} -3 \\ 1 \\ 2t \end{pmatrix}$ and $\mathbf{v} = \begin{pmatrix} 1 \\ t \\ -1 \end{pmatrix}$ are perpendicular, what is the value of t?

A $\quad -3$

B $\quad -2$

C $\quad \dfrac{2}{3}$

D $\quad 1$

[Turn over

8. The volume of a sphere is given by the formula $V = \frac{4}{3}\pi r^3$.

   What is the rate of change of V with respect to r, at $r = 2$?

   A $\dfrac{16\pi}{3}$

   B $\dfrac{32\pi}{3}$

   C 16π

   D 32π

9. The diagram shows the curve with equation of the form $y = \cos(x + a) + b$ for $0 \leq x \leq 2\pi$.

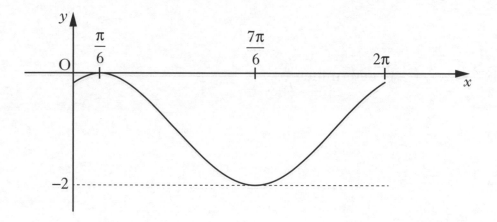

   What is the equation of this curve?

   A $y = \cos\left(x - \dfrac{\pi}{6}\right) - 1$

   B $y = \cos\left(x - \dfrac{\pi}{6}\right) + 1$

   C $y = \cos\left(x + \dfrac{\pi}{6}\right) - 1$

   D $y = \cos\left(x + \dfrac{\pi}{6}\right) + 1$

10. The diagram shows a square-based pyramid P,QRST.

$\overrightarrow{TS}$, $\overrightarrow{TQ}$ and $\overrightarrow{TP}$ represent **f**, **g** and **h** respectively.

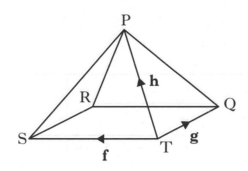

Express $\overrightarrow{RP}$ in terms of **f**, **g** and **h**.

A $-\mathbf{f} + \mathbf{g} - \mathbf{h}$

B $-\mathbf{f} - \mathbf{g} + \mathbf{h}$

C $\mathbf{f} - \mathbf{g} - \mathbf{h}$

D $\mathbf{f} + \mathbf{g} + \mathbf{h}$

11. Find $\int \left(\dfrac{1}{6x^2} \right) dx,\ x \neq 0$.

A $-12x^{-3} + c$

B $-6x^{-1} + c$

C $-\dfrac{1}{3} x^{-3} + c$

D $-\dfrac{1}{6} x^{-1} + c$

12. Find the maximum value of

$$2 - 3\sin\left(x - \frac{\pi}{3} \right)$$

and the value of x where this occurs in the interval $0 \leq x \leq 2\pi$.

	max value	x
A	−1	$\dfrac{11\pi}{6}$
B	5	$\dfrac{11\pi}{6}$
C	−1	$\dfrac{5\pi}{6}$
D	5	$\dfrac{5\pi}{6}$

13. A parabola intersects the axes at $x = -2$, $x = -1$ and $y = 6$, as shown in the diagram.

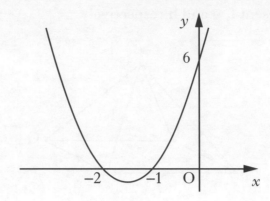

What is the equation of the parabola?

A $y = 6(x - 1)(x - 2)$

B $y = 6(x + 1)(x + 2)$

C $y = 3(x - 1)(x - 2)$

D $y = 3(x + 1)(x + 2)$

14. Find $\int (2x - 1)^{\frac{1}{2}} \, dx$ where $x > \frac{1}{2}$.

A $\frac{1}{3}(2x - 1)^{\frac{3}{2}} + c$

B $\frac{1}{2}(2x - 1)^{-\frac{1}{2}} + c$

C $\frac{1}{2}(2x - 1)^{\frac{3}{2}} + c$

D $\frac{1}{3}(2x - 1)^{-\frac{1}{2}} + c$

15. If $\mathbf{u} = k \begin{pmatrix} 3 \\ -1 \\ 0 \end{pmatrix}$, where $k > 0$ and $\mathbf{u}$ is a unit vector, determine the value of k.

A $\frac{1}{2}$

B $\frac{1}{8}$

C $\frac{1}{\sqrt{2}}$

D $\frac{1}{\sqrt{10}}$

16. If $y = 3\cos^4 x$, find $\dfrac{dy}{dx}$.

A $12\cos^3 x \sin x$

B $12\cos^3 x$

C $-12\cos^3 x \sin x$

D $-12\sin^3 x$

17. Given that $\mathbf{a} = \begin{pmatrix} 3 \\ 4 \\ 0 \end{pmatrix}$ and $\mathbf{a}.(\mathbf{a}+\mathbf{b})=7$, what is the value of $\mathbf{a}.\mathbf{b}$?

A $\dfrac{7}{25}$

B $-\dfrac{18}{5}$

C -6

D -18

18. The graph of $y = f(x)$ shown has stationary points at $(0, p)$ and (q, r).

Here are two statements about $f(x)$:

(1) $f(x) < 0$ for $s < x < t$;

(2) $f'(x) < 0$ for $x < q$.

Which of the following is true?

A   Neither statement is correct.

B   Only statement (1) is correct.

C   Only statement (2) is correct.

D   Both statements are correct.

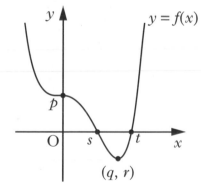

[Turn over

19. Solve $6 - x - x^2 < 0$.

   A $-3 < x < 2$

   B $x < -3, x > 2$

   C $-2 < x < 3$

   D $x < -2, x > 3$

20. Simplify $\dfrac{\log_b 9a^2}{\log_b 3a}$, where $a > 0$ and $b > 0$.

   A 2

   B $3a$

   C $\log_b 3a$

   D $\log_b(9a^2 - 3a)$

[*END OF SECTION A*]

SECTION B

Marks

ALL questions should be attempted.

21. (*a*) (i) Show that $(x - 4)$ is a factor of $x^3 - 5x^2 + 2x + 8$.

(ii) Factorise $x^3 - 5x^2 + 2x + 8$ fully.

(iii) Solve $x^3 - 5x^2 + 2x + 8 = 0$. **6**

(*b*) The diagram shows the curve with equation $y = x^3 - 5x^2 + 2x + 8$.

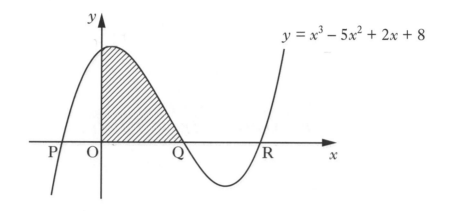

The curve crosses the *x*-axis at P, Q and R.

Determine the shaded area. **6**

22. (*a*) The expression $\cos x - \sqrt{3}\sin x$ can be written in the form $k\cos(x + a)$ where $k > 0$ and $0 \le a < 2\pi$.

Calculate the values of k and a. **4**

(*b*) Find the points of intersection of the graph of $y = \cos x - \sqrt{3}\sin x$ with the *x* and *y* axes, in the interval $0 \le x \le 2\pi$. **3**

[Turn over for Question 23 on *Page twelve*

Marks

23. (*a*) Find the equation of ℓ_1, the perpendicular bisector of the line joining P(3, −3) to Q(−1, 9).   **4**

(*b*) Find the equation of ℓ_2 which is parallel to PQ and passes through R(1, −2).   **2**

(*c*) Find the point of intersection of ℓ_1 and ℓ_2.   **3**

(*d*) Hence find the shortest distance between PQ and ℓ_2.   **2**

[END OF SECTION B]

[END OF QUESTION PAPER]

X100/12/03

NATIONAL
QUALIFICATIONS
2012

MONDAY, 21 MAY
2.50 PM – 4.00 PM

MATHEMATICS
HIGHER
Paper 2

Read Carefully

1　**Calculators may be used in this paper.**

2　Full credit will be given only where the solution contains appropriate working.

3　Answers obtained by readings from scale drawings will not receive any credit.

FORMULAE LIST

Circle:

The equation $x^2 + y^2 + 2gx + 2fy + c = 0$ represents a circle centre $(-g, -f)$ and radius $\sqrt{g^2 + f^2 - c}$.

The equation $(x - a)^2 + (y - b)^2 = r^2$ represents a circle centre (a, b) and radius r.

Scalar Product: $\mathbf{a}.\mathbf{b} = |\mathbf{a}||\mathbf{b}| \cos \theta$, where θ is the angle between $\mathbf{a}$ and $\mathbf{b}$

or $\mathbf{a}.\mathbf{b} = a_1b_1 + a_2b_2 + a_3b_3$ where $\mathbf{a} = \begin{pmatrix} a_1 \\ a_2 \\ a_3 \end{pmatrix}$ and $\mathbf{b} = \begin{pmatrix} b_1 \\ b_2 \\ b_3 \end{pmatrix}$.

Trigonometric formulae:

$$\sin (A \pm B) = \sin A \cos B \pm \cos A \sin B$$
$$\cos (A \pm B) = \cos A \cos B \mp \sin A \sin B$$
$$\sin 2A = 2\sin A \cos A$$
$$\cos 2A = \cos^2 A - \sin^2 A$$
$$= 2\cos^2 A - 1$$
$$= 1 - 2\sin^2 A$$

Table of standard derivatives:

$f(x)$	$f'(x)$
$\sin ax$	$a \cos ax$
$\cos ax$	$-a \sin ax$

Table of standard integrals:

$f(x)$	$\int f(x)dx$
$\sin ax$	$-\dfrac{1}{a} \cos ax + C$
$\cos ax$	$\dfrac{1}{a} \sin ax + C$

ALL questions should be attempted.   *Marks*

1. Functions f and g are defined on the set of real numbers by

    - $f(x) = x^2 + 3$
    - $g(x) = x + 4.$

    (*a*) Find expressions for:

      (i) $f(g(x))$;

      (ii) $g(f(x))$.   **3**

    (*b*) Show that $f(g(x)) + g(f(x)) = 0$ has no real roots.   **3**

2. (*a*) Relative to a suitable set of coordinate axes, Diagram 1 shows the line $2x - y + 5 = 0$ intersecting the circle $x^2 + y^2 - 6x - 2y - 30 = 0$ at the points P and Q.

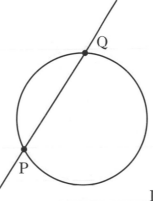

Diagram 1

Find the coordinates of P and Q.   **6**

    (*b*) Diagram 2 shows the circle from (*a*) and a second congruent circle, which also passes through P and Q.

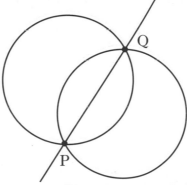

Diagram 2

                                                                          6

Determine the equation of this second circle.

Marks

3. A function f is defined on the domain $0 \le x \le 3$ by $f(x) = x^3 - 2x^2 - 4x + 6$.

   Determine the maximum and minimum values of f.   **7**

4. The diagram below shows the graph of a quartic $y = h(x)$, with stationary points at $x = 0$ and $x = 2$.

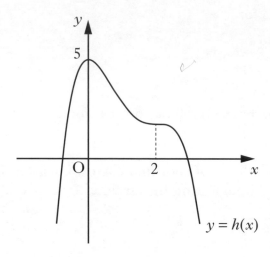

   On separate diagrams sketch the graphs of:

   (a) $y = h'(x)$;   **3**

   (b) $y = 2 - h'(x)$.   **3**

5. A is the point $(3, -3, 0)$, B is $(2, -3, 1)$ and C is $(4, k, 0)$.

   (a) (i)   Express $\overrightarrow{BA}$ and $\overrightarrow{BC}$ in component form.

        (ii) Show that $\cos \hat{ABC} = \dfrac{3}{\sqrt{2(k^2 + 6k + 14)}}$.   **7**

   (b) If angle ABC = $30°$, find the possible values of k.   **5**

Marks

6. For $0 < x < \frac{\pi}{2}$, sequences can be generated using the recurrence relation

$$u_{n+1} = (\sin x)u_n + \cos 2x, \text{ with } u_0 = 1.$$

    (a) Why do these sequences have a limit?   **2**

    (b) The limit of one sequence generated by this recurrence relation is $\frac{1}{2}\sin x$.

        Find the value(s) of x.   **7**

7. The diagram shows the curves with equations $y = 4^x$ and $y = 3^{2-x}$.

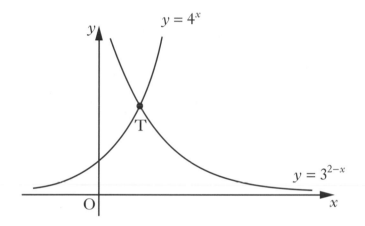

The graphs intersect at the point T.

    (a) Show that the x – coordinate of T can be written in the form $\dfrac{\log_a p}{\log_a q}$,

        for all $a > 1$.   **6**

    (b) Calculate the y – coordinate of T.   **2**

[END OF QUESTION PAPER]

[BLANK PAGE]

HIGHER

2013

[BLANK PAGE]

X100/12/02

NATIONAL
QUALIFICATIONS
2013

WEDNESDAY, 22 MAY
1.00 PM – 2.30 PM

MATHEMATICS
HIGHER
Paper 1
(Non-calculator)

Read carefully

Calculators may <u>NOT</u> be used in this paper.

Section A – Questions 1–20 (40 marks)

Instructions for completion of **Section A** are given on Page two.

For this section of the examination you must use an **HB pencil**.

Section B (30 marks)

1   Full credit will be given only where the solution contains appropriate working.

2   Answers obtained by readings from scale drawings will not receive any credit.

Read carefully

1 Check that the answer sheet provided is for **Mathematics Higher (Section A)**.

2 For this section of the examination you must use an **HB pencil** and, where necessary, an eraser.

3 Check that the answer sheet you have been given has **your name**, **date of birth**, **SCN** (Scottish Candidate Number) and **Centre Name** printed on it.

Do not change any of these details.

4 If any of this information is wrong, tell the Invigilator immediately.

5 If this information is correct, **print** your name and seat number in the boxes provided.

6 The answer to each question is **either** A, B, C or D. Decide what your answer is, then, using your pencil, put a horizontal line in the space provided (see sample question below).

7 There is **only one correct** answer to each question.

8 Rough working should **not** be done on your answer sheet.

9 At the end of the exam, put the **answer sheet for Section A inside the front cover of your answer book**.

Sample Question

A curve has equation $y = x^3 - 4x$.

What is the gradient at the point where x = 2?

      A   8

      B   1

      C   0

      D − 4

The correct answer is **A**—8. The answer **A** has been clearly marked in **pencil** with a horizontal line (see below).

    A   **B**   **C**   **D**

Changing an answer

If you decide to change your answer, carefully erase your first answer and, using your pencil, fill in the answer you want. The answer below has been changed to **D**.

    A   **B**   **C**   **D**

FORMULAE LIST

Circle:

The equation $x^2 + y^2 + 2gx + 2fy + c = 0$ represents a circle centre $(-g, -f)$ and radius $\sqrt{g^2 + f^2 - c}$.

The equation $(x - a)^2 + (y - b)^2 = r^2$ represents a circle centre (a, b) and radius r.

Scalar Product: $\mathbf{a}.\mathbf{b} = |\mathbf{a}||\mathbf{b}| \cos \theta$, where θ is the angle between $\mathbf{a}$ and $\mathbf{b}$

or $\mathbf{a}.\mathbf{b} = a_1b_1 + a_2b_2 + a_3b_3$ where $\mathbf{a} = \begin{pmatrix} a_1 \\ a_2 \\ a_3 \end{pmatrix}$ and $\mathbf{b} = \begin{pmatrix} b_1 \\ b_2 \\ b_3 \end{pmatrix}$.

Trigonometric formulae:

$\sin (A \pm B) = \sin A \cos B \pm \cos A \sin B$

$\cos (A \pm B) = \cos A \cos B \mp \sin A \sin B$

$\sin 2A = 2\sin A \cos A$

$\cos 2A = \cos^2 A - \sin^2 A$

$= 2\cos^2 A - 1$

$= 1 - 2\sin^2 A$

Table of standard derivatives:

$f(x)$	$f'(x)$
$\sin ax$	$a \cos ax$
$\cos ax$	$-a \sin ax$

Table of standard integrals:

$f(x)$	$\int f(x)dx$
$\sin ax$	$-\dfrac{1}{a} \cos ax + C$
$\cos ax$	$\dfrac{1}{a} \sin ax + C$

[Turn over

SECTION A

ALL questions should be attempted.

1. The functions f and g are defined by $f(x) = x^2 + 1$ and $g(x) = 3x - 4$, on the set of real numbers.

   Find $g(f(x))$.

   A $3x^2 - 1$

   B $9x^2 - 15$

   C $9x^2 + 17$

   D $3x^3 - 4x^2 + 3x - 4$

2. The point P (5, 12) lies on the curve with equation $y = x^2 - 4x + 7$.

   What is the gradient of the tangent to this curve at P?

   A   2

   B   6

   C   12

   D   13

3. Calculate the discriminant of the quadratic equation $2x^2 + 4x + 5 = 0$.

   A   −32

   B   −24

   C   48

   D   56

4. Which of the following shows the graph of $y = 4\cos 2x - 1$, for $0 \leq x \leq \pi$?

A

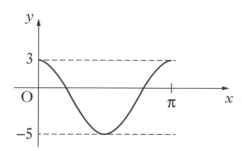

B

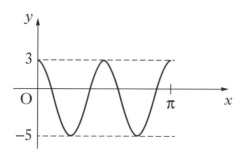

C

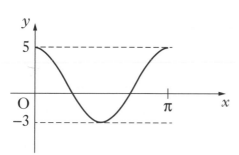

D

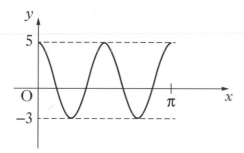

[Turn over

5. The line L passes through the point (−2, −1) and is parallel to the line with equation $5x + 3y - 6 = 0$.

   What is the equation of L?

   A $3x + 5y - 11 = 0$

   B $3x + 5y + 11 = 0$

   C $5x + 3y - 13 = 0$

   D $5x + 3y + 13 = 0$

6. What is the remainder when $x^3 + 3x^2 - 5x - 6$ is divided by $(x - 2)$?

   A 0

   B 3

   C 4

   D 8

7. Find $\int x(3x + 2)\, dx$.

   A $x^3 + c$

   B $x^3 + x^2 + c$

   C $\frac{1}{2}x^2\left(\frac{3}{2}x^2 + 2x\right) + c$

   D $3x^2 + 2x + c$

8. A sequence is defined by the recurrence relation $u_{n+1} = 0 \cdot 1 u_n + 8$, with $u_1 = 11$.

Here are two statements about this sequence:

(1) $u_0 = 9 \cdot 1$;

(2) The sequence has a limit as $n \longrightarrow \infty$.

Which of the following is true?

A   Neither statement is correct.

B   Only statement (1) is correct.

C   Only statement (2) is correct.

D   Both statements are correct.

9. The diagram shows a right-angled triangle with sides and angles as marked.

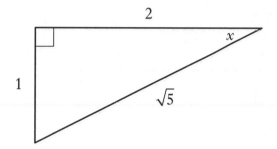

Find the value of $\sin 2x$.

A $\dfrac{4}{5}$

B $\dfrac{2}{5}$

C $\dfrac{2}{\sqrt{5}}$

D $\dfrac{1}{\sqrt{5}}$

10. If $0 < a < 90$, which of the following is equivalent to $\cos(270 - a)°$?

A $\cos a°$

B $\sin a°$

C $-\cos a°$

D $-\sin a°$

11. The diagram shows a cubic curve with equation $y = f(x)$.

Which of the following diagrams could show the curve with equation $y = -f(x - k)$, $k > 0$?

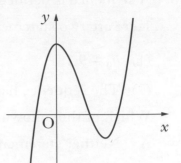

A

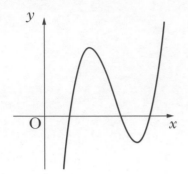

B

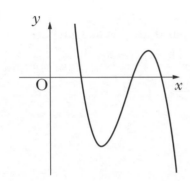

C

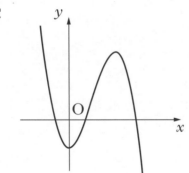

D

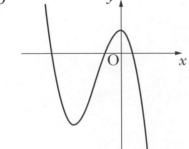

12. If $\mathbf{f} = 3\mathbf{i} + 2\mathbf{k}$ and $\mathbf{g} = 2\mathbf{i} + 4\mathbf{j} + 3\mathbf{k}$, find $|\mathbf{f} + \mathbf{g}|$.

A $\sqrt{14}$ units

B $\sqrt{42}$ units

C $\sqrt{66}$ units

D $\sqrt{70}$ units

13. A function f is defined on a suitable domain by $f(x) = \dfrac{x+2}{x^2 - 7x + 12}$.

What value(s) of x cannot be in this domain?

A 3 and 4

B -3 and -4

C -2

D 0

14. Given that $|\mathbf{a}| = 3$, $|\mathbf{b}| = 2$ and $\mathbf{a}.\mathbf{b} = 5$, what is the value of $\mathbf{a}.(\mathbf{a} + \mathbf{b})$?

A 11

B 14

C 15

D 21

15. Solve $\tan\left(\dfrac{x}{2}\right) = -1$ for $0 \le x < 2\pi$.

A $\dfrac{\pi}{2}$

B $\dfrac{7\pi}{8}$

C $\dfrac{3\pi}{2}$

D $\dfrac{15\pi}{8}$

[Turn over

16. Find $\int (1-6x)^{-\frac{1}{2}}dx$ where $x < \frac{1}{6}$.

A $\frac{1}{9}(1-6x)^{-\frac{3}{2}}+c$

B $3(1-6x)^{-\frac{3}{2}}+c$

C $-\frac{1}{3}(1-6x)^{\frac{1}{2}}+c$

D $-3(1-6x)^{\frac{1}{2}}+c$

17. The diagram shows a curve with equation of the form $y = kx(x + a)^2$, which passes through the points $(-2, 0)$, $(0, 0)$ and $(1, 3)$.

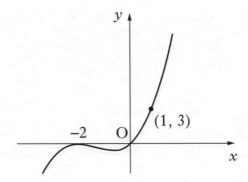

What are the values of a and k?

	a	k
A	−2	$\frac{1}{3}$
B	−2	3
C	2	$\frac{1}{3}$
D	2	3

18. Given that $y = \sin(x^2 - 3)$, find $\dfrac{dy}{dx}$.

A $\sin 2x$

B $\cos 2x$

C $2x \sin(x^2 - 3)$

D $2x \cos(x^2 - 3)$

19. Solve $1 - 2x - 3x^2 > 0$, where x is a real number.

A $x < -1$ or $x > \dfrac{1}{3}$

B $-1 < x < \dfrac{1}{3}$

C $x < -\dfrac{1}{3}$ or $x > 1$

D $-\dfrac{1}{3} < x < 1$

20. The graph of $\log_3 y$ plotted against x is a line through the origin with gradient 2, as shown.

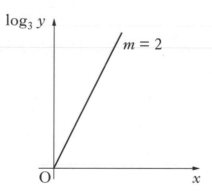

Express y in terms of x.

A $y = 2x$

B $y = 9x$

C $y = 6^x$

D $y = 9^x$

[*END OF SECTION A*]

[**Turn over for SECTION B**
on *Page twelve*

SECTION B

ALL questions should be attempted.

Marks

21. Express $2x^2 + 12x + 1$ in the form $a(x + b)^2 + c$.   **3**

22. A circle C_1 has equation $x^2 + y^2 + 2x + 4y - 27 = 0$.

    (*a*) Write down the centre and calculate the radius of C_1.   **2**

    (*b*) The point P(3, 2) lies on the circle C_1.

        Find the equation of the tangent at P.   **3**

    (*c*) A second circle C_2 has centre (10, −1). The radius of C_2 is half of the radius of C_1.

        Show that the equation of C_2 is $x^2 + y^2 - 20x + 2y + 93 = 0$.   **3**

    (*d*) Show that the tangent found in part (*b*) is also a tangent to circle C_2.   **4**

23. (*a*) The expression $\sqrt{3}\sin x° - \cos x°$ can be written in the form $k\,\sin(x - a)°$, where $k > 0$ and $0 \le a < 360$.

        Calculate the values of k and a.   **4**

    (*b*) Determine the maximum value of $4 + 5\cos x° - 5\sqrt{3}\sin x°$, where $0 \le x < 360$.   **2**

24. (*a*)   (i) Show that the points A(−7, −8, 1), T(3, 2, 5) and B(18, 17, 11) are collinear.

        (ii) Find the ratio in which T divides AB.   **4**

    (*b*) The point C lies on the *x*-axis.

        If TB and TC are perpendicular, find the co-ordinates of C.   **5**

[END OF SECTION B]

[END OF QUESTION PAPER]

X100/12/03

NATIONAL
QUALIFICATIONS
2013

WEDNESDAY, 22 MAY
2.50 PM – 4.00 PM

MATHEMATICS
HIGHER
Paper 2

Read carefully

1   **Calculators may be used in this paper.**

2   Full credit will be given only where the solution contains appropriate working.

3   Answers obtained by readings from scale drawings will not receive any credit.

FORMULAE LIST

Circle:

The equation $x^2 + y^2 + 2gx + 2fy + c = 0$ represents a circle centre $(-g, -f)$ and radius $\sqrt{g^2 + f^2 - c}$.

The equation $(x - a)^2 + (y - b)^2 = r^2$ represents a circle centre (a, b) and radius r.

Scalar Product: $\mathbf{a}.\mathbf{b} = |\mathbf{a}||\mathbf{b}| \cos \theta$, where θ is the angle between $\mathbf{a}$ and $\mathbf{b}$

or $\mathbf{a}.\mathbf{b} = a_1b_1 + a_2b_2 + a_3b_3$ where $\mathbf{a} = \begin{pmatrix} a_1 \\ a_2 \\ a_3 \end{pmatrix}$ and $\mathbf{b} = \begin{pmatrix} b_1 \\ b_2 \\ b_3 \end{pmatrix}$.

Trigonometric formulae:

$$\sin (A \pm B) = \sin A \cos B \pm \cos A \sin B$$
$$\cos (A \pm B) = \cos A \cos B \mp \sin A \sin B$$
$$\sin 2A = 2\sin A \cos A$$
$$\cos 2A = \cos^2 A - \sin^2 A$$
$$= 2\cos^2 A - 1$$
$$= 1 - 2\sin^2 A$$

Table of standard derivatives:

$f(x)$	$f'(x)$
$\sin ax$	$a \cos ax$
$\cos ax$	$-a \sin ax$

Table of standard integrals:

$f(x)$	$\int f(x)dx$
$\sin ax$	$-\frac{1}{a} \cos ax + C$
$\cos ax$	$\frac{1}{a} \sin ax + C$

ALL questions should be attempted.   *Marks*

1. The first three terms of a sequence are 4, 7 and 16.

    The sequence is generated by the recurrence relation

    $$u_{n+1} = mu_n + c, \text{ with } u_1 = 4.$$

    Find the values of m and c.   4

2. The diagram shows rectangle PQRS with P(7, 2) and Q(5, 6).

    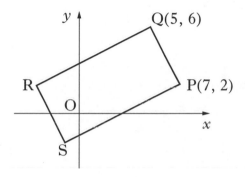

    (a) Find the equation of QR.   3

    (b) The line from P with the equation $x + 3y = 13$ intersects QR at T.

    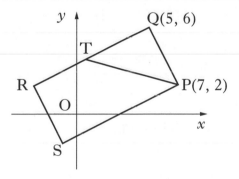

    Find the coordinates of T.   3

    (c) Given that T is the midpoint of QR, find the coordinates of R and S.   3

[Turn over

Marks

3. (*a*) Given that $(x - 1)$ is a factor of $x^3 + 3x^2 + x - 5$, factorise this cubic fully.   **4**

(*b*) Show that the curve with equation

$$y = x^4 + 4x^3 + 2x^2 - 20x + 3$$

has only one stationary point.

Find the *x*-coordinate and determine the nature of this point.   **5**

4. The line with equation $y = 2x + 3$ is a tangent to the curve with equation $y = x^3 + 3x^2 + 2x + 3$ at A(0, 3), as shown in the diagram.

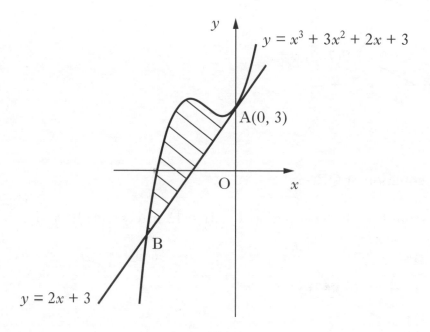

The line meets the curve again at B.

Show that B is the point $(-3, -3)$ and find the area enclosed by the line and the curve.   **6**

5. Solve the equation

$$\log_5(3 - 2x) + \log_5(2 + x) = 1, \text{ where } x \text{ is a real number.}$$ **4**

Marks

6. Given that $\int_0^a 5\sin 3x \, dx = \dfrac{10}{3}$, $0 \le a < \pi$,

calculate the value of a.   **5**

7. A manufacturer is asked to design an open-ended shelter, as shown, subject to the following conditions.

Condition 1

The frame of a shelter is to be made of rods of two different lengths:

- x metres for top and bottom edges;
- y metres for each sloping edge.

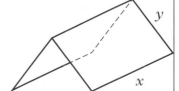

Condition 2

The frame is to be covered by a rectangular sheet of material.

The total area of the sheet is $24\,\text{m}^2$.

(a) Show that the total length, L metres, of the rods used in a shelter is given by

$$L = 3x + \frac{48}{x}.$$

    3

(b) These rods cost £8·25 per metre.

To minimise production costs, the total length of rods used for a frame should be as small as possible.

   (i) Find the value of x for which L is a minimum.

   (ii) Calculate the minimum cost of a frame.   **7**

8. Solve algebraically the equation

$$\sin 2x = 2\cos^2 x \qquad \text{for } 0 \le x < 2\pi$$

    6

[Turn over for Question 9 on *Page six*

9. The concentration of the pesticide, *Xpesto*, in soil can be modelled by the equation   *Marks*

$$P_t = P_0 e^{-kt}$$

where:

- P_0 is the initial concentration;
- P_t is the concentration at time t;
- t is the time, in days, after the application of the pesticide.

(a) Once in the soil, the half-life of a pesticide is the time taken for its concentration to be reduced to one half of its initial value.

   If the half-life of *Xpesto* is 25 days, find the value of k to 2 significant figures.   **4**

(b) Eighty days after the initial application, what is the percentage decrease in concentration of *Xpesto*?   **3**

[END OF QUESTION PAPER]

[BLANK PAGE]

X100/12/02

NATIONAL
QUALIFICATIONS
2014

TUESDAY, 6 MAY
1.00 PM – 2.30 PM

MATHEMATICS
HIGHER
Paper 1
(Non-calculator)

Read carefully

Calculators may <u>NOT</u> be used in this paper.

Section A – Questions 1–20 (40 marks)

Instructions for completion of **Section A** are given on Page two.

For this section of the examination you must use an **HB pencil**.

Section B (30 marks)

1   Full credit will be given only where the solution contains appropriate working.

2   Answers obtained by readings from scale drawings will not receive any credit.

Read carefully

1 Check that the answer sheet provided is for **Mathematics Higher (Section A)**.

2 For this section of the examination you must use an **HB pencil** and, where necessary, an eraser.

3 Check that the answer sheet you have been given has **your name**, **date of birth**, **SCN** (Scottish Candidate Number) and **Centre Name** printed on it.

   Do not change any of these details.

4 If any of this information is wrong, tell the Invigilator immediately.

5 If this information is correct, **print** your name and seat number in the boxes provided.

6 The answer to each question is A, B, C or D. Decide what your answer is, then, using your pencil, put a horizontal line in the space provided (see sample question below).

7 There is **only one correct** answer to each question.

8 Rough working should **not** be done on your answer sheet.

9 At the end of the exam, put the **answer sheet for Section A inside the front cover of your answer book**.

Sample Question

A curve has equation $y = x^3 - 4x$.

What is the gradient at the point where $x = 2$?

    A   8

    B   1

    C   0

    D -4

The correct answer is **A**—8. The answer **A** has been clearly marked in **pencil** with a horizontal line (see below).

A   B   C   D

Changing an answer

If you decide to change your answer, carefully erase your first answer and, using your pencil, fill in the answer you want. The answer below has been changed to **D**.

A   B   C   D

FORMULAE LIST

Circle:

The equation $x^2 + y^2 + 2gx + 2fy + c = 0$ represents a circle centre $(-g, -f)$ and radius $\sqrt{g^2 + f^2 - c}$.

The equation $(x - a)^2 + (y - b)^2 = r^2$ represents a circle centre (a, b) and radius r.

Scalar Product: $\mathbf{a}.\mathbf{b} = |\mathbf{a}||\mathbf{b}| \cos \theta$, where θ is the angle between $\mathbf{a}$ and $\mathbf{b}$

or $\mathbf{a}.\mathbf{b} = a_1b_1 + a_2b_2 + a_3b_3$ where $\mathbf{a} = \begin{pmatrix} a_1 \\ a_2 \\ a_3 \end{pmatrix}$ and $\mathbf{b} = \begin{pmatrix} b_1 \\ b_2 \\ b_3 \end{pmatrix}$.

Trigonometric formulae:

$$\sin (A \pm B) = \sin A \cos B \pm \cos A \sin B$$
$$\cos (A \pm B) = \cos A \cos B \mp \sin A \sin B$$
$$\sin 2A = 2\sin A \cos A$$
$$\cos 2A = \cos^2 A - \sin^2 A$$
$$= 2\cos^2 A - 1$$
$$= 1 - 2\sin^2 A$$

Table of standard derivatives:

$f(x)$	$f'(x)$
$\sin ax$	$a \cos ax$
$\cos ax$	$-a \sin ax$

Table of standard integrals:

$f(x)$	$\int f(x)dx$
$\sin ax$	$-\dfrac{1}{a} \cos ax + c$
$\cos ax$	$\dfrac{1}{a} \sin ax + c$

[Turn over

SECTION A

ALL questions should be attempted.

1. A sequence is defined by the recurrence relation $u_{n+1} = \frac{1}{3}u_n + 1$, with $u_2 = 15$.
   What is the value of u_4?

   A $2\frac{1}{9}$

   B $2\frac{1}{3}$

   C 3

   D 30

2. The diagram shows a circle with centre C(1, 2) and the tangent at T(3, −1).

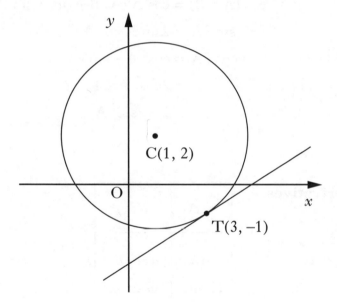

   What is the gradient of this tangent?

   A $\frac{1}{4}$

   B $\frac{2}{3}$

   C $\frac{3}{2}$

   D 4

3. If $\log_4 12 - \log_4 x = \log_4 6$, what is the value of x?

A   2

B   6

C   18

D   72

4. If $3\sin x - 4\cos x$ is written in the form $k\cos(x - a)$, what are the values of $k\cos a$ and $k\sin a$?

	$k\cos a$	$k\sin a$
A	-3	4
B	3	-4
C	4	-3
D	-4	3

5. Find $\int (2x+9)^5\,dx$.

A $10\,(2x + 9)^4 + c$

B $\frac{1}{4}\,(2x + 9)^4 + c$

C $10\,(2x + 9)^6 + c$

D $\frac{1}{12}\,(2x + 9)^6 + c$

[Turn over

6. Given that $u = \begin{pmatrix} -3 \\ 1 \\ 0 \end{pmatrix}$ and $v = \begin{pmatrix} 1 \\ -1 \\ 2 \end{pmatrix}$, find $2u - 3v$ in component form.

A $\begin{pmatrix} -9 \\ 5 \\ -6 \end{pmatrix}$

B $\begin{pmatrix} -9 \\ -1 \\ -4 \end{pmatrix}$

C $\begin{pmatrix} -3 \\ -1 \\ 6 \end{pmatrix}$

D $\begin{pmatrix} 11 \\ -5 \\ 4 \end{pmatrix}$

7. A right-angled triangle has sides and angles as shown in the diagram.

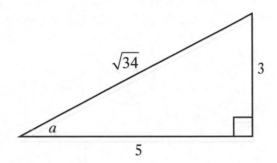

What is the value of $\sin 2a$?

A $\dfrac{8}{17}$

B $\dfrac{3}{\sqrt{34}}$

C $\dfrac{15}{17}$

D $\dfrac{6}{\sqrt{34}}$

8. What is the derivative of $\left(4-9x^4\right)^{\frac{1}{2}}$?

A $-\frac{9}{2}\left(4-9x^4\right)^{-\frac{1}{2}}$

B $\frac{1}{2}\left(4-9x^{-4}\right)^{-\frac{1}{2}}$

C $2\left(4-9x^4\right)^{-\frac{1}{2}}$

D $-18x^3\left(4-9x^4\right)^{-\frac{1}{2}}$

9. $\sin x+\sqrt{3}\cos x$ can be written as $2\cos\left(x-\frac{\pi}{6}\right)$.

The maximum value of $\sin x+\sqrt{3}\cos x$ is 2.

What is the maximum value of $5\sin 2x+5\sqrt{3}\cos 2x$?

A   20

B   10

C   5

D   2

10. A sequence is defined by the recurrence relation

$u_{n+1}=(k-2)u_n+5$ with $u_0=3$.

For what values of k does this sequence have a limit as $n\to\infty$?

A $-3<k<-1$

B $-1<k<1$

C $1<k<3$

D $k<3$

[Turn over

11. The diagram shows part of the graph of $y = f(x)$.

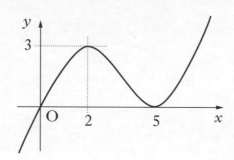

Which of the following diagrams could be the graph of $y = 2f(x) + 1$?

A

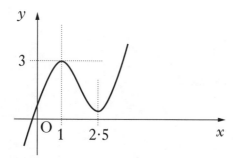

B

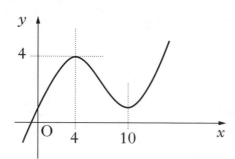

C

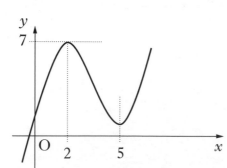

D

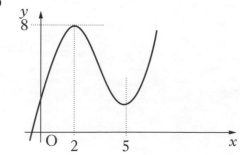

12. A function f, defined on a suitable domain, is given by $f(x) = \dfrac{6x}{x^2 + 6x - 16}$.

What restrictions are there on the domain of f?

A $x \neq -8$ or $x \neq 2$

B $x \neq -4$ or $x \neq 4$

C $x \neq 0$

D $x \neq 10$ or $x \neq 16$

13. What is the value of $\sin\left(\dfrac{\pi}{3}\right) - \cos\left(\dfrac{5\pi}{4}\right)$?

A $\dfrac{\sqrt{3}}{2} - \dfrac{1}{\sqrt{2}}$

B $\dfrac{\sqrt{3}}{2} + \dfrac{1}{\sqrt{2}}$

C $\dfrac{1}{2} - \dfrac{1}{\sqrt{2}}$

D $\dfrac{1}{2} + \dfrac{1}{\sqrt{2}}$

14. The vectors $\boldsymbol{u} = \begin{pmatrix} 1 \\ k \\ k \end{pmatrix}$ and $\boldsymbol{v} = \begin{pmatrix} -6 \\ 2 \\ 5 \end{pmatrix}$ are perpendicular.

What is the value of k?

A $\dfrac{-6}{7}$

B -1

C 1

D $\dfrac{6}{7}$

[Turn over

15. The diagram shows a cubic curve passing through (–1, 0), (2, 0) and (0, –8).

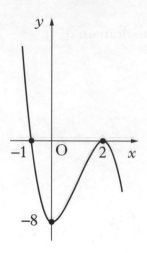

What is the equation of the curve?

A $y = -2(x + 1)^2(x + 2)$

B $y = -2(x + 1)(x - 2)^2$

C $y = 4(x + 1)(x - 2)$

D $y = -8(x + 1)(x - 2)^2$

16. The unit vectors $\boldsymbol{a}$ and $\boldsymbol{b}$ are such that $\boldsymbol{a}.\boldsymbol{b} = \frac{2}{3}$. Determine the value of $\boldsymbol{a}.(\boldsymbol{a} + 2\boldsymbol{b})$.

A $\frac{2}{3}$

B $\frac{4}{3}$

C $\frac{7}{3}$

D   3

17. $3x^2 + 12x + 17$ is expressed in the form $3(x + p)^2 + q$.
What is the value of q?

A   1

B   5

C   17

D   –19

18. What is the value of $1 - 2\sin^2 15°$?

  A $\dfrac{1}{2}$

  B $\dfrac{3}{4}$

  C $\dfrac{\sqrt{3}}{2}$

  D $\dfrac{7}{8}$

19. The diagram shows a regular hexagon PQRSTW.

$\overrightarrow{PW}$ and $\overrightarrow{PQ}$ represent vectors $\boldsymbol{u}$ and $\boldsymbol{v}$ respectively.

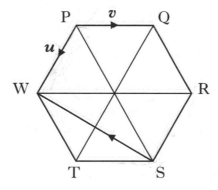

What is $\overrightarrow{SW}$ in terms of $\boldsymbol{u}$ and $\boldsymbol{v}$?

  A $-\boldsymbol{u} - 2\boldsymbol{v}$

  B $-\boldsymbol{u} - \boldsymbol{v}$

  C $\boldsymbol{u} - \boldsymbol{v}$

  D $\boldsymbol{u} + 2\boldsymbol{v}$

20. Evaluate $2 - \log_5 \dfrac{1}{25}$.

  A -3

  B 0

  C $\dfrac{3}{2}$

  D 4

[END OF SECTION A]

SECTION B

ALL questions should be attempted.

Marks

21. A curve has equation $y = 3x^2 - x^3$.

    (a) Find the coordinates of the stationary points on this curve and determine their nature.   **6**

    (b) State the coordinates of the points where the curve meets the coordinate axes and sketch the curve.   **2**

22. For the polynomial $6x^3 + 7x^2 + ax + b$,

    - $x + 1$ is a factor
    - 72 is the remainder when it is divided by $x - 2$.

    (a) Determine the values of a and b.   **4**

    (b) Hence factorise the polynomial completely.   **3**

23. (a) Find P and Q, the points of intersection of the line $y = 3x - 5$ and the circle C_1 with equation $x^2 + y^2 + 2x - 4y - 15 = 0$.   **4**

    (b) T is the centre of C_1.

    Show that PT and QT are perpendicular.   **3**

    (c) A second circle C_2 passes through P, Q and T.

    Find the equation of C_2.   **3**

24. Two variables, x and y, are related by the equation

Marks

$$y = ka^x.$$

When $\log_9 y$ is plotted against x, a straight line passing through the points $(0, 2)$ and $(6, 5)$ is obtained, as shown in the diagram.

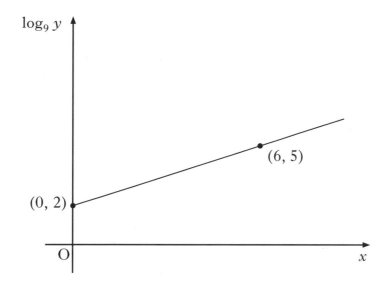

Find the values of k and a.

5

[*END OF SECTION B*]

[*END OF QUESTION PAPER*]

$$y = mx + c$$

$$\log_9 y = \frac{1}{2}x + 2$$

$$y = {\scriptstyle 1}9^{(\frac{1}{2}x + 2)}$$

$$y = a$$

[BLANK PAGE]

X100/12/03

NATIONAL
QUALIFICATIONS
2014

TUESDAY, 6 MAY
2.50 PM – 4.00 PM

MATHEMATICS
HIGHER
Paper 2

Read carefully

1 **Calculators may be used in this paper.**

2 Full credit will be given only where the solution contains appropriate working.

3 Answers obtained by readings from scale drawings will not receive any credit.

FORMULAE LIST

Circle:

The equation $x^2 + y^2 + 2gx + 2fy + c = 0$ represents a circle centre $(-g, -f)$ and radius $\sqrt{g^2 + f^2 - c}$.

The equation $(x - a)^2 + (y - b)^2 = r^2$ represents a circle centre (a, b) and radius r.

Scalar Product: $\quad \mathbf{a}.\mathbf{b} = |\mathbf{a}|\,|\mathbf{b}| \cos \theta$, where θ is the angle between $\mathbf{a}$ and $\mathbf{b}$

$$\text{or} \quad \mathbf{a}.\mathbf{b} = a_1b_1 + a_2b_2 + a_3b_3 \text{ where } \mathbf{a} = \begin{pmatrix} a_1 \\ a_2 \\ a_3 \end{pmatrix} \text{ and } \mathbf{b} = \begin{pmatrix} b_1 \\ b_2 \\ b_3 \end{pmatrix}.$$

Trigonometric formulae:

$$\sin (A \pm B) = \sin A \cos B \pm \cos A \sin B$$
$$\cos (A \pm B) = \cos A \cos B \mp \sin A \sin B$$
$$\sin 2A = 2\sin A \cos A$$
$$\cos 2A = \cos^2 A - \sin^2 A$$
$$= 2\cos^2 A - 1$$
$$= 1 - 2\sin^2 A$$

Table of standard derivatives:

$f(x)$	$f'(x)$
$\sin ax$	$a \cos ax$
$\cos ax$	$-a \sin ax$

Table of standard integrals:

$f(x)$	$\int f(x)dx$
$\sin ax$	$-\dfrac{1}{a} \cos ax + c$
$\cos ax$	$\dfrac{1}{a} \sin ax + c$

ALL questions should be attempted.

Marks

1. A(3, 0), B(5, 2) and the origin are the vertices of a triangle as shown in the diagram.

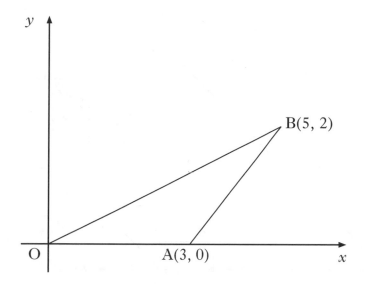

(a) Obtain the equation of the perpendicular bisector of AB. **4**

(b) The median from A has equation $y + 2x = 6$.

Find T, the point of intersection of this median and the perpendicular bisector of AB. **2**

(c) Calculate the angle that AT makes with the positive direction of the x-axis. **2**

2. A curve has equation $y = x^4 - 2x^3 + 5$.

Find the equation of the tangent to this curve at the point where $x = 2$. **4**

3. Functions f and g are defined on suitable domains by

$$f(x) = x(x - 1) + q \text{ and } g(x) = x + 3.$$

(a) Find an expression for $f(g(x))$. **2**

(b) Hence, find the value of q such that the equation $f(g(x)) = 0$
has equal roots. **4**

[Turn over

Marks

4. Six identical cuboids are placed with their edges parallel to the coordinate axes as shown in the diagram.

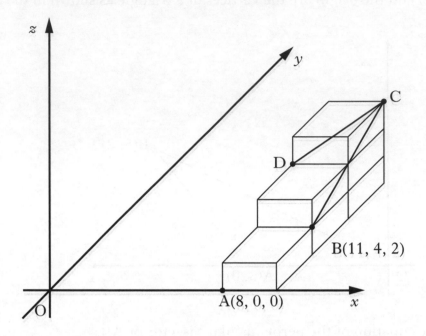

A and B are the points (8, 0, 0) and (11, 4, 2) respectively.

(a) State the coordinates of C and D.   2

(b) Determine the components of $\overrightarrow{CB}$ and $\overrightarrow{CD}$.   2

(c) Find the size of the angle BCD.   5

5. Given that $\int_{4}^{t} (3x+4)^{-\frac{1}{2}}\, dx = 2$, find the value of t.   5

6. Solve the equation

$$\sin x - 2\cos 2x = 1 \qquad \text{for } 0 \le x < 2\pi.$$ 5

Marks

7. Land enclosed between a path and a railway line is being developed for housing. This land is represented by the shaded area shown in Diagram 1.

   - The path is represented by a parabola with equation $y = 6x - x^2$.
   - The railway is represented by a line with equation $y = 2x$.
   - One square unit in the diagram represents $300\,m^2$ of land.

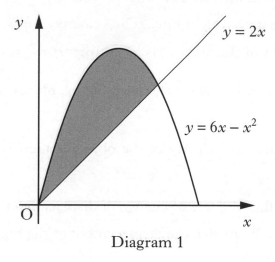

Diagram 1

(a) Calculate the area of land being developed.   **5**

(b) A road is built parallel to the railway line and is a tangent to the path as shown in Diagram 2.

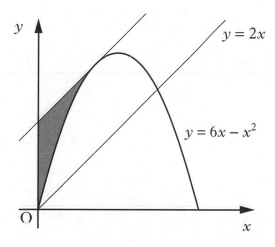

Diagram 2

It is decided that the land, represented by the shaded area in Diagram 2, will become a car park.

Calculate the area of the car park.   **5**

[**Turn over**

Marks

8. Given that the equation

$$x^2 + y^2 - 2px - 4py + 3p + 2 = 0$$

   represents a circle, determine the range of values of p.   **5**

9. Acceleration is defined as the rate of change of velocity.

   An object is travelling in a straight line. The velocity, v m/s, of this object,

   t seconds after the start of the motion, is given by $v(t) = 8\cos(2t - \frac{\pi}{2})$.

   (a) Find a formula for $a(t)$, the acceleration of this object, t seconds after the start
       of the motion.   **3**

   (b) Determine whether the velocity of the object is increasing or decreasing when
       $t = 10$.   **2**

   (c) Velocity is defined as the rate of change of displacement.

       Determine a formula for $s(t)$, the displacement of the object, given that
       $s(t) = 4$ when $t = 0$.   **3**

[END OF QUESTION PAPER]

MATHEMATICS HIGHER
PAPER 1
2010

SECTION A

1. A	**2.** C	**3.** D	**4.** A	**5.** B
6. D	**7.** C	**8.** B	**9.** C	**10.** B
11. D	**12.** A	**13.** B	**14.** C	**15.** C
16. A	**17.** B	**18.** B	**19.** C	**20.** A

SECTION B

21. (a) $2x + 5y - 72 = 0$

(b) Show that $2 \times 6 + 5 \times 12 - 72 = 0$ so T lies on line BQ.

(c) BT : TQ is $2 : 1$

22. (a) $f(x) = (x - 1)(x - 1)(2x + 5)$

or

$f(x) = (x - 1)^2(2x + 5)$

(b) $x = -\dfrac{5}{2}$ **or** $x = 1$

(c) G$(1, -1)$

(d) H$\left(-\dfrac{5}{2}, -8\right)$

23. (a) (i) $m = \dfrac{3}{2}$ and $m = \tan a$ so $\tan a = \dfrac{3}{2}$

(ii) $\sin a = \dfrac{3}{\sqrt{13}}$

(b) $\sin b = \dfrac{3}{5}$ and $\cos b = \dfrac{4}{5}$

(c) (i) $\sin(a - b) = \dfrac{6}{5\sqrt{13}}$

(ii) $\sin(b - a) = -\dfrac{6}{5\sqrt{13}}$

MATHEMATICS HIGHER
PAPER 2
2010

1. (a) M$(0, 1, 0)$ and N$(4, 2, 2)$

(b) $\overrightarrow{VM} = \begin{pmatrix} 0 \\ -1 \\ -3 \end{pmatrix}$ and $\overrightarrow{VN} = \begin{pmatrix} 4 \\ 0 \\ -1 \end{pmatrix}$

(c) $\angle$MVN = $76 \cdot 7°$ **or** $1 \cdot 339$ radians

2. (a) $k = 13$ and $a = 22 \cdot 6$ (to 1 d.p.)

(b) (i) Maximum value 13 and minimum value -13

(ii) Maximum occurs at $x = 337 \cdot 4$
Minimum occurs at $x = 157 \cdot 4$

3. (a) (i) Substitute expression for y from line into equation of circle
$$x^2 + (3 - x)^2 + 14x + 4(3 - x) - 19 = 0$$
leading to $2x^2 + 4x + 2 = 0$ and line being tangent to circle.

(ii) P$(-1, 4)$

(b) $(x - 1)^2 + (y - 6)^2 = 8$

4. $\{2 \cdot 419, 3 \cdot 864\}$

5. (a) (i) From T$(0, 4)$, length of PQ is
$$10 - x^2 - 4 = 6 - x^2$$

(ii) Area: $2x \times (6 - x^2) = 12x - 2x^3$

(b) Maxium area $8\sqrt{2}$ ($\approx 11 \cdot 3$) square units
(This occurs at $x = \sqrt{2}$ ($\approx 1 \cdot 4$))

6. (a) From $y = (2x - 9)^{\frac{1}{2}}$ then $m_{\text{tangent}} = \dfrac{dy}{dx} = (2x - 9)^{-\frac{1}{2}}$

When $x = 9$ then $m_{\text{tangent}} = \dfrac{dy}{dx} = (18 - 9)^{-\frac{1}{2}} = \dfrac{1}{3}$

and $y = (2x - 9)^{\frac{1}{2}} = (18 - 9)^{\frac{1}{2}} = 3$
(**NB** Need to use equation of curve to get this value of 3)
This leads to $y - 3 = \dfrac{1}{3}(x - 9)$ and so $y = \dfrac{1}{3}x$

(b) A$\left(\dfrac{9}{2}, 0\right)$

(c) Two main methods:
Shaded area = area of large triangle − area under curve from $\dfrac{9}{2}$ to 9.

or

Shaded area = area of small triangle + area between line and curve from $\dfrac{9}{2}$ to 9.

This leads to shaded area $\dfrac{9}{2}$ square units.

7. (a) $\log_4 x = $ P

$x = 4^{\text{P}}$

$\log_{16} x = \log_{16} 4^{\text{P}}$

$= \text{P} \log_{16} 4$

$= \dfrac{1}{2}\text{P}$

(b) $\log_3 x + \log_9 x = 12$

$\log_3 x + \frac{1}{2}\log_3 x = 12$

$\frac{3}{2}\log_3 x = 12$

$\log_3 x = 8$

$x = 3^8$ (6561)

MATHEMATICS HIGHER PAPER 1 2011

SECTION A

1. C	2. B	3. D	4. D	5. A
6. C	7. D	8. A	9. B	10. D
11. D	12. C	13. C	14. B	15. B
16. A	17. A	18. C	19. C	20. D

SECTION B

21. (a) $3x - y - 9 = 0$

(b)   E(5, 6)

(c) (i) $2x + y - 16 = 0$

(ii) e.g. Substitute E(5, 6) into $2x + y - 16$ and show the result is 0

22. (a) (i) (2, 0)

(ii) (0, $-$ 2)

(b) Maximum turning point at $\left(\frac{1}{3}, -\frac{50}{27}\right)$

Minimum turning point at (1, $-$ 2)

(c) (i)

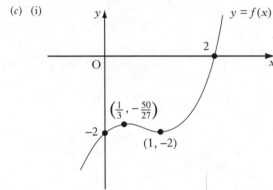

(ii)

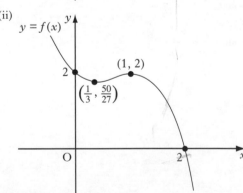

23. (a) $\{0, 60, 300\}$

(b) Using the fact $\cos 4x = \cos(2 \times 2x)$ leading to $\{0, 30, 150, 180, 210, 330\}$

MATHEMATICS HIGHER
PAPER 2
2011

1. (a) B(4, 4, 0)

(b) $\overrightarrow{DB} = \begin{pmatrix} 2 \\ 2 \\ -6 \end{pmatrix}$ and $\overrightarrow{DM} = \begin{pmatrix} 0 \\ -2 \\ -6 \end{pmatrix}$

(c) 40·3° or 0·703 rads

2. (a) $g(f(x)) = g(x^3 - 1)$
$= 3x^3 - 2$

(b) $g(f(x)) + xh(x) = 3x^3 - 2 + 4x^2 - 5x$
$= 3x^3 + 4x^2 - 5x - 2$

(c) $(x - 1)(3x + 1)(x + 2)$

(d) $\left\{ -2, -\frac{1}{3}, 1 \right\}$

3. (a) $u_1 = 8$ and $u_2 = -4$

(b) $p = 2$ and $q = -3$

(c) (i) Limit is 0.

(ii) 2 lies outside the interval $-1 < a < 1$, where $a = 2$

4. Shaded area: $\int_{-2}^{0} (x^3 - x^2 - 4x + 4) - (2x + 4) \, dx +$

$\int_{0}^{3} (2x + 4) - (x^3 - x^2 - 4x + 4) \, dx$

$= \frac{253}{12}$

5. $k = 32$ and $n = \frac{1}{2}$

6. (a) $R = \sqrt{34}$ and $a = 5·253$

(b) $t = 0·6$

7. $-23 < p < 13$

MATHEMATICS HIGHER
PAPER 1
2012

SECTION A

1. C	**2.** D	**3.** B	**4.** B	**5.** A
6. C	**7.** A	**8.** C	**9.** A	**10.** B
11. D	**12.** B	**13.** D	**14.** A	**15.** D
16. C	**17.** D	**18.** B	**19.** B	**20.** A

SECTION B

21. (a) (i) Show $f(4) = 0$ either by synthetic division or direct substitution of 4 into cubic expression.
(Need to link 0 to the factor whatever method is used to gain communication mark.)

(ii) $(x - 4)(x - 2)(x + 1)$

(iii) $\{-1, 2, 4\}$

(b) Area is given by

$\int_{0}^{2} (x^3 - 5x^2 + 2x + 8) \, dx = \frac{32}{3}$ square units.

22. (a) $k = 2$ and $a = \frac{\pi}{3}$

(Your solution must contain the working:
$\cos x - \sqrt{3} \sin x = k \cos x \cos a - k \sin x \sin a$ **and**
then equating coefficients $k \cos a = 1$ and $k \sin a = \sqrt{3}$.)

(b) y-axis intercept : $(0, 1)$.

x-axis intercepts : $\left(\frac{\pi}{6}, 0 \right)$ and $\left(\frac{7\pi}{6}, 0 \right)$

23. (a) $x - 3y + 8 = 0$

(b) $3x + y - 1 = 0$

(c) $\left(-\frac{1}{2}, \frac{5}{2} \right)$

(d) Distance between $(1, 3)$ and $\left(-\frac{1}{2}, \frac{5}{2} \right)$, which is $\sqrt{\frac{5}{2}}$ units.

MATHEMATICS HIGHER
PAPER 2
2012

1. (a) (i) $f(x + 4) = (x + 4)^2 + 3 = x^2 + 8x + 19$.

    (ii) $g(x^2 + 3) = x^2 + 3 + 4 = x^2 + 7$.

  (b) **Either**
    $f(g(x)) + g(f(x)) = 0$
    $2x^2 + 8x + 26 = 0$
    $\therefore b^2 - 4ac = 8^2 - 4 \times 2 \times 26 = -144$
    or
    $f(g(x)) + g(f(x)) = 0$
    $2x^2 + 8x + 26 = 0$ leading to $x^2 + 4x + 13 = 0$
    $\therefore b^2 - 4ac = 4^2 - 4 \times 1 \times 13 = -36$

    Therefore $b^2 - 4ac < 0$ and so no real roots.

2. (a) Substitute expression for y from line into equation of circle
    $x^2 + (2x + 5)^2 - 6x - 2(2x + 5) - 30 = 0$
    leading to $5x^2 + 10x - 15 = 0$
    and the points P$(-3, -1)$ and Q$(1, 7)$.

  (b) $(x + 5)^2 + (y - 5)^2 = 40$

3. Maximum value is 6 and minimum value is -2.

4. (a)

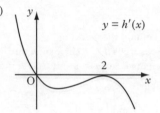

$y = h'(x)$

  (b)

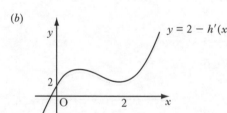

$y = 2 - h'(x)$

5. (a) (i) $\overrightarrow{BA} = \begin{pmatrix} 1 \\ 0 \\ -1 \end{pmatrix}$ and $\overrightarrow{BC} = \begin{pmatrix} 2 \\ k + 3 \\ -1 \end{pmatrix}$

    (ii) Using

$$\cos ABC = \frac{\overrightarrow{BA}.\overrightarrow{BC}}{|\overrightarrow{BA}||\overrightarrow{BC}|}$$

$$= \frac{1 \times 2 + 0 \times (k + 3) + (-1) \times (-1)}{\sqrt{1^2 + 0^2 + (-1)^2} \ \sqrt{2^2 + (k + 3)^2 + (-1)^2}}$$

$$= \frac{3}{\sqrt{2} \ \sqrt{k^2 + 6k + 14}}$$

$$= \frac{3}{\sqrt{2(k^2 + 6k + 14)}}$$

  (b) Solving $\dfrac{3}{\sqrt{2(k^2 + 6k + 14)}} = \cos 30°$

    leads to $k = -2$ or -4.

6. (a) For a limit to exist we require $-1 < \sin x < 1$.

    In the interval $0 < x < \dfrac{\pi}{2}$, $0 < \sin x < 1$.

    So limit exists.

  (b) Solving either $\dfrac{1}{2} \sin x = \dfrac{\cos 2x}{1 - \sin x}$

    or $\dfrac{1}{2} \sin x = \sin x \times \dfrac{1}{2} \sin x + \cos 2x$

    Replace $\cos 2x$ by $1 - 2\sin^2 x$, leading to $x \approx 0{\cdot}73$ as the only valid solution in the given interval.

7. (a) At point of intersection T
$$4^x = 3^{2-x}$$
$$\log_a (4^x) = \log_a (3^{2-x})$$
$$x \log_a 4 = (2 - x) \log_a 3$$
$$x\log_a 4 + x \log_a 3 = 2 \log_a 3$$
$$x(\log_a 4 + \log_a 3) = \log_a 3^2$$
$$x \log_a 12 = \log_a 9$$
$$x = \frac{\log_a 9}{\log_a 12}$$

  (b) To find y-coordinate use:
$$y = 4^{\frac{\log_a 9}{\log_a 12}}$$

    Choosing **any positive base** for a gives $y \approx 3{\cdot}4$.

MATHEMATICS HIGHER PAPER 1 2013

SECTION A

1. A	2. B	3. B	4. A	5. D
6. C	7. B	8. C	9. A	10. D
11. B	12. C	13. A	14. B	15. C
16. C	17. C	18. D	19. B	20. D

SECTION B

21. $2(x^2 + 6x + 1)$

$= 2[(x + 3)^2 - 9] + 1$
$= 2(x + 3)^2 - 17$

or

$ax^2 + 2abx + ab^2 + c$
$a = 2 \quad 2ab = 12 \quad ab^2 + c = 1$
$2(x + 3)^2 - 17$

22. (a) centre $(-1, -2)$
radius is $\sqrt{32}$

(b) $m_{\text{radius}} = 1$

$m_{\text{tangent}} = 1$

$y - 2 = -1(x - 3)$

(c) $\sqrt{32} = \frac{1}{2} \times 2\sqrt{8} = \sqrt{8}$

$(x - 10)^2 + (y + 1)^2 = (\sqrt{8})^2$
$x^2 - 20x + 100 + y^2 + 2y + 1 = 8$
giving $x^2 + y^2 - 20x + 2y + 93 = 0$

(d) Substituting for y
$x^2 + (5 - x)^2 - 20x + 2(5 - x) + 93$

$2x^2 - 32x + 128 = 0$

$2(x - 8)^2 = 0$
equal roots
$\Rightarrow$ tangent

or

$(-32)^2 - 4 \times 2 \times 128$
$b^2 - 4ac = 0$
$\Rightarrow$ tangent

or

Substituting for x
$(5 - y)^2 + y^2 - 20(5 - y) + 2y + 93 = 0$
$2y^2 + 12y + 18 = 0$

$2(y + 3)^2 = 0$
equal roots
$\Rightarrow$ tangent

or

$12^2 - 4 \times 2 \times 18$
$b^2 - 4ac = 0$
$\Rightarrow$ tangent

23. (a) $\sqrt{3} \sin x - \cos x = k \sin x° \cos a° - k \cos x° \sin a°$

$k \cos a° = \sqrt{3}$ and $k \sin a° = 1$
$k = 2$
$a = 30$

(b) $4 - 5 \times 2 \sin (x - 30)°$
$4 - (-10)$, maximum is 14

24. (a) (i) $\overrightarrow{AT} = \begin{pmatrix} 10 \\ 10 \\ 4 \end{pmatrix}$ or $\overrightarrow{TB} = \begin{pmatrix} 15 \\ 15 \\ 6 \end{pmatrix}$

$\overrightarrow{AT} = \frac{2}{3} \overrightarrow{TB}$ or equivalent

$\overrightarrow{AT}$ and $\overrightarrow{TB}$ are parallel and since there is a common point A, B and T are collinear

(ii) 2:3

(b) point lies on the x-axis $(c, 0, 0)$

$\overrightarrow{TC} = \begin{pmatrix} c - 3 \\ -2 \\ -5 \end{pmatrix}$

Method 1: using scalar product equal to zero

$\overrightarrow{TB} . \overrightarrow{TC} = 0$

$15(c - 3) + 15 \times (-2) + 6 \times (-5) = 0$

$c = 7$

or

Method 2: using Pythagoras' theorem

$\left| \overrightarrow{TC} \right| = \sqrt{(c - 3)^2 + 4 + 25}$

$\left| \overrightarrow{TB} \right| = \sqrt{486}$

$\left| \overrightarrow{BC} \right| = \sqrt{(c - 18)^2 + 289 + 121}$

$c = 7$

MATHEMATICS HIGHER
PAPER 2
2013

1. $7 = 4m + c$

$16 = 7m + c$

$7m + c = 16$
$4m + c = 7$

$m = 3, c = -5$

2. (a) $m_{PQ} = -2$

$m_{QR} = \dfrac{1}{2}$

$y - 6 = \dfrac{1}{2}(x - 5)$

(b) $x + 3y = 13$ and $x - 2y = -7$

solving simultaneously gives

$x = 1$ **and** $y = 4$; T(1, 4)

(c) $\overrightarrow{QT} = \begin{pmatrix} -4 \\ -2 \end{pmatrix}$ $\begin{pmatrix} 1 \\ 4 \end{pmatrix} + \begin{pmatrix} -4 \\ -2 \end{pmatrix} = \begin{pmatrix} -3 \\ 2 \end{pmatrix}$

R(−3, 2)

$\overrightarrow{RS} = \overrightarrow{QP} = \begin{pmatrix} 2 \\ -4 \end{pmatrix}$ $\begin{pmatrix} -3 \\ 2 \end{pmatrix} + \begin{pmatrix} 2 \\ -4 \end{pmatrix} = \begin{pmatrix} -1 \\ -2 \end{pmatrix}$

S(−1, −2)

3. (a) Use a method of division to obtain

$x^3 + 3x^2 + x - 5 = (x - 1)(x^2 + 4x + 5)$

$b^2 - 4ac = 16 - 20 < 0$

$\Rightarrow$ cubic will not factorise further

(b) differentiate and equate to zero

$4x^3 + 12x^2 + 4x - 20 = 0$

$4(x - 1)(x^2 + 4x + 5) = 0$

$x = 1$

justify nature (nature table or second derivative)
and minimum

4. $(-3)^3 + 3(-3)^2 + 2(-3) + 3 = -3$

and $2(-3) + 3 = -3$

$\displaystyle\int_{-3}^{0} (x^3 + 3x^2 + 2x + 3) - (2x + 3)\,dx$

$= \left[\frac{1}{4}x^4 + x^3 \right]_{-3}^{0}$

$= 0 - \left(\frac{1}{4}(-3)^4 + (-3)^3 \right)$

$= \frac{27}{4}$ units^2

5. $\log_5 [(3 - 2x)(2 + x)] = 1$

$(3 - 2x)(2 + x) = 5^1$

$2x^2 + x - 1 = 0$

$x = \dfrac{1}{2}$, $x = -1$

6. $\left[\frac{-5}{3} \cos 3x \right]$

$\frac{-5}{3} \cos 3a + \frac{5}{3} \cos 0$

$\frac{-5}{3} \cos 3a + \frac{5}{3} = \frac{10}{3}$

$\cos 3a = -1$

$a = \frac{\pi}{3}$

7. (a) $L = 3x + 4y$

$y = \dfrac{24}{2x}$

$L = 3x + 4 \times \dfrac{24}{2x} = 3x + \dfrac{48}{x}$

(b) (i) $3 - \dfrac{48}{x^2} = 0$

$x = 4$

justify minimum (2nd derivative or nature table)
$L = 24$

(ii) cost $24 \times £8·25 = £198$

8. $2 \sin x \cos x - 2\cos^2 x = 0$

$2 \cos x (\sin x - \cos x) = 0$

$\cos x = 0$ and $\sin x = \cos x$

$x = \dfrac{\pi}{2}, \dfrac{3\pi}{2}$ $x = \dfrac{\pi}{4}, \dfrac{5\pi}{4}$

9. (a) $\dfrac{1}{2} P_0 = P_0 e^{-25k}$

$e^{-25k} = \dfrac{1}{2}$

$\log_e \dfrac{1}{2} = -25k$

$k \approx 0·028$

(b) $P_t = P_0 e^{-80 \times 0·028}$

$P_t \approx 0·1065 P_0$

$\Rightarrow$ percentage decrease is $100 - 10.65 \approx 89\%$

MATHEMATICS HIGHER
PAPER 1
2014

SECTION A

1. C	**2.** B	**3.** A	**4.** D	**5.** D
6. A	**7.** C	**8.** D	**9.** B	**10.** C
11. C	**12.** A	**13.** B	**14.** D	**15.** B
16. C	**17.** B	**18.** C	**19.** A	**20.** D

SECTION B

21. (a) $= 6x....$ **or** $= ....-3x^2$

$6x - 3x^2 = 0$

$x = 0, 2$

$y = 0, 4$

use 2nd derivature or nature table

min. at $(0, 0)$ and max. at $(2,4)$

(b) $3x^2 - x^3 = 0$; $(3, 0)$ $(0, 0)$

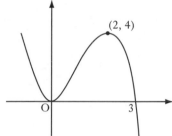

22. (a) $6(-1)^3 + 7(-1)^2 + a(-1) + b = 0$, $a - b = 1$

$6(2)^3 + 7(2)^2 + a(2) + b = 72$, $2a + b = -4$

$a = -1$

$b = -2$

Alternative Method

$$\begin{array}{c|cccc}
-1 & 6 & 7 & a & b \\
 & & -6 & -1 & -a+1 \\
\hline
 & 6 & 1 & a-1 & b-a+1=0
\end{array}$$

$$\begin{array}{c|cccc}
2 & 6 & 7 & a & b \\
 & & 12 & 38 & 2a+76 \\
\hline
 & 6 & 19 & a+38 & 2a+b+76=72
\end{array}$$

(b) Divide $(6x^3 + 7x^2 - x - 2)$ by $(x + 1)$ to get

$6x^3 + 7x^2 - x - 2 = (x + 1) (6x^2 + x - 2)$

$= (x + 1) (3x + 2) (2x - 1)$

23. (a) $x^2 + (3x - 5)^2 + 2x - 4(3x - 5) - 15 = 0$

$10x^2 - 40x + 30 = 0$

P $(1, -2)$

Q $(3, 4)$

Labels for P and Q may be reversed

(b) T $(-1,2)$

$m_{PT} = -2$, $m_{QT} - \dfrac{1}{2}$

$-2 \times \dfrac{1}{2} = -1$

$\Rightarrow$ PT is perpendicular to QT

Alternative Method

T $(-1,2)$

$\begin{pmatrix} -2 \\ 4 \end{pmatrix}$ and $\begin{pmatrix} -4 \\ -2 \end{pmatrix}$

$\begin{pmatrix} -2 \\ 4 \end{pmatrix} . \begin{pmatrix} -4 \\ -2 \end{pmatrix} = -2 \times -4 + 4 \times -2 = 0$

PT is perpendicular to QT

(c) centre $(2, 1)$

radius $= \sqrt{10}$

$(x - 2)^2 + (y - 1)^2 = 10$

Alternative Method: substituting points into equation of circle

$x^2 + y^2 + 2gx + 2fy + c = 0$

$25 + 6g + 8f + c = 0$

$5 + 2g - 4f + c = 0$

$5 - 2g + 4f + c = 0$

$f = -1, g = -2, c = -5$

24. Method 1

$\log_9 y = \log_9 ka^x$

$\log_9 y = \log_9 k + \log_9 a^x$

$\log_9 y = \log_9 k + x \log_9 a$

$\log_9 k = 2$, $k = 81$ or $k = 9^2 = 81$

$\log_9 a = \dfrac{1}{2}$, $a = 3$ or $a = 9^{½} = 3$

Method 2

$\log_9 y = \dfrac{1}{2}x + 2$

$y = 9^{½x+2}$

$y = 9^{½x} 9^2$

$k = 81$

$a = 3$

Method 3

at $(0, 2)$, $\log_9 y = 2$

$\qquad\qquad y = 9^2 = 81$

$81 = ka^0$

$\Rightarrow k = 81$

at $(6, 5)$, $\log_9 y = 5$

$\qquad\qquad y = 9^5$

$9^5 = ka^6$

$9^5 = 81a^6$

$\Rightarrow a^6 = 9^3 = 3^6$

$\Rightarrow a = 3$

MATHEMATICS HIGHER
PAPER 2
2014

1. (a) $m_{AB} = 1$

$m_{perp} = -1$

midpoint of AB (4,1)

$y - 1 = -1(x - 4)$

(b) $y + 2x = 6$

$y + x = 5$

$x = 1, y = 4$

(c) $\tan \theta = -2$

$116 \cdot 6°$

or $2 \cdot 03$ radians

2. $\dfrac{dy}{dx} = 4x^3 - 6x^2$

$m = 8$

$y = 5$

$y - 5 = 8(x - 2)$

3. (a) $f(x + 3)$

$= (x + 3)(x + 2) + q$

or

$= (x + 3)^2 - (x + 3) + q$

(b) **Method 1**

$x^2 + 5x + 6 + q = 0$

$b^2 - 4ac = 5^2 - 4 \times 1 \times (6 + q)$

$\Rightarrow 25 - 24 - 4q = 0$

$q = \dfrac{1}{4}$

Method 2

$x^2 + 5x + 6 + q = 0$

$\left(x + \dfrac{5}{2}\right)^2 - \dfrac{25}{4} + 6 + q = 0$

$-\dfrac{25}{4} + 6 + q = 0$

$q = \dfrac{1}{4}$

Method 3

$f(g(x)) = x^2 + 5x + 6 + q = 0$

equal roots so touches x-axis at SP

$\Rightarrow \dfrac{dy}{dx} = 2x + 5 = 0$

$x = -\dfrac{5}{2}$

$\dfrac{25}{4} - \dfrac{25}{2} + 6 + q = 0$

$q = \dfrac{1}{4}$

4. (a) C(11,12,6)

D(8,8,4)

(b) $\overrightarrow{CB} = \begin{pmatrix} 0 \\ -8 \\ -4 \end{pmatrix}$, $\overrightarrow{CD} = \begin{pmatrix} -3 \\ -4 \\ -2 \end{pmatrix}$

(c) $\cos \hat{BCD} = \dfrac{\overrightarrow{CB}.\overrightarrow{CD}}{\left|\overrightarrow{CB}\right|\left|\overrightarrow{CD}\right|}$

$\overrightarrow{CB}.\overrightarrow{CD} = 40$

$\left|\overrightarrow{CB}\right| = \sqrt{80}$

$\left|\overrightarrow{CD}\right| = \sqrt{29}$

$\hat{BCD} = 33 \cdot 9°$

5. $\dfrac{1}{\frac{1}{2}} (......)^{\frac{1}{2}} \times \dfrac{1}{3}$

$= \dfrac{2}{3} (3x + 4)^{\frac{1}{2}}$

$\dfrac{2}{3} (3t + 4)^{\frac{1}{2}} - \dfrac{2}{3} (3(4) + 4)^{\frac{1}{2}} = 2$

$(3t + 4)^{\frac{1}{2}} = 7$

$t = 15$

6. $\sin x - 2(1 - 2\sin^2 x) = 1$

$4 \sin^2 x + \sin x - 3 = 0$

$(4 \sin x - 3)(\sin x + 1) = 0$

$\sin x = \dfrac{3}{4}$ and $\sin x = -1$

$x = 0 \cdot 848, 2 \cdot 29$ and $\dfrac{3\pi}{2}$

7. (a) $2x = 6x - x^2 \Rightarrow x = 0, x = 4$

$\int ((6x - x^2) - 2x)dx$

$= 2x^2 - \dfrac{1}{3} x^3$

$= 10\dfrac{2}{3}$

Area $= 10\dfrac{2}{3} \times 300 = 3200\text{m}^2$

(b) $\dfrac{dy}{dx} = 6 - 2x = 2$

$x = 2, y = 8$

$y = 2x + 4$

$\left[\left(x^2 + 4x\right) - \left(3x^2 - \dfrac{1}{3} x^3\right)\right]_0^2$

$= \dfrac{8}{3}$

Area $= 800\text{m}^2$

8. $g = -p, f = -2p, c = -3p + 2$

radius $= g^2 + f^2 - c = 5p^2 - 3p - 2$

$g^2 + f^2 - c > 0$

$(5p + 2)(p - 1) = 0 \Rightarrow p = -\dfrac{2}{5}, p = 1$

$p < -\dfrac{2}{5}, p > 1$

9. (a) $a = v'(t)$

$= -8\sin \left(2t - \dfrac{\pi}{2}\right) \times 2$

$a(t) = -16\sin \left(2t - \dfrac{\pi}{2}\right)$

(b) $a(10) = 6 \cdot 53$

$a(10) > 0$ therefore increasing

[radians must be used]

(c) $s(t) = \int v(t)dt$

$s(t) = 4\sin \left(2t - \dfrac{\pi}{2}\right) + c$

$c = 8$ so $s(t) = 4\sin \left(2t - \dfrac{\pi}{2}\right) + 8$